AF619224

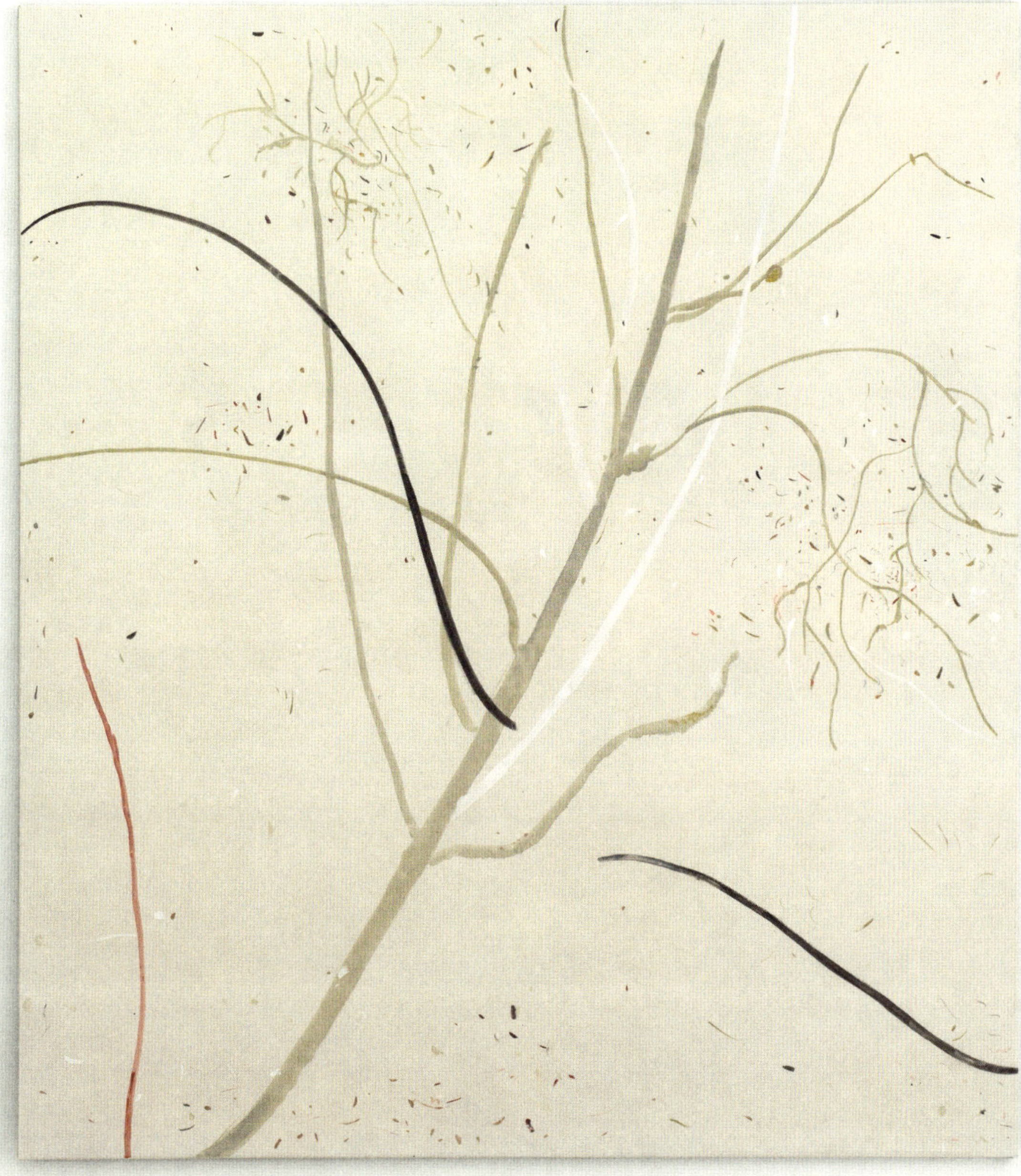

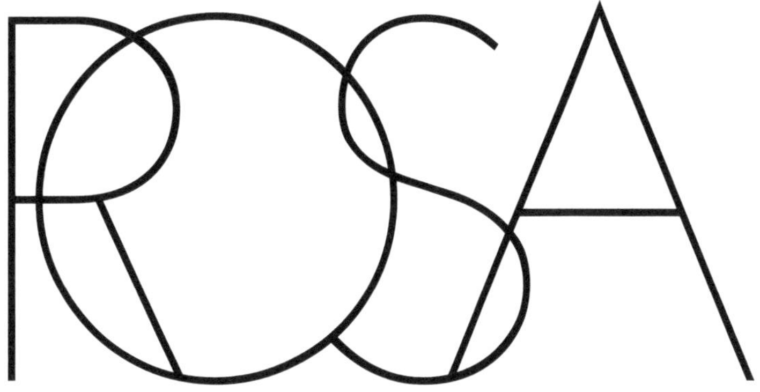

Rosilene Luduvico & Sabrina Fritsch

DISTANZ

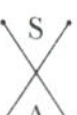

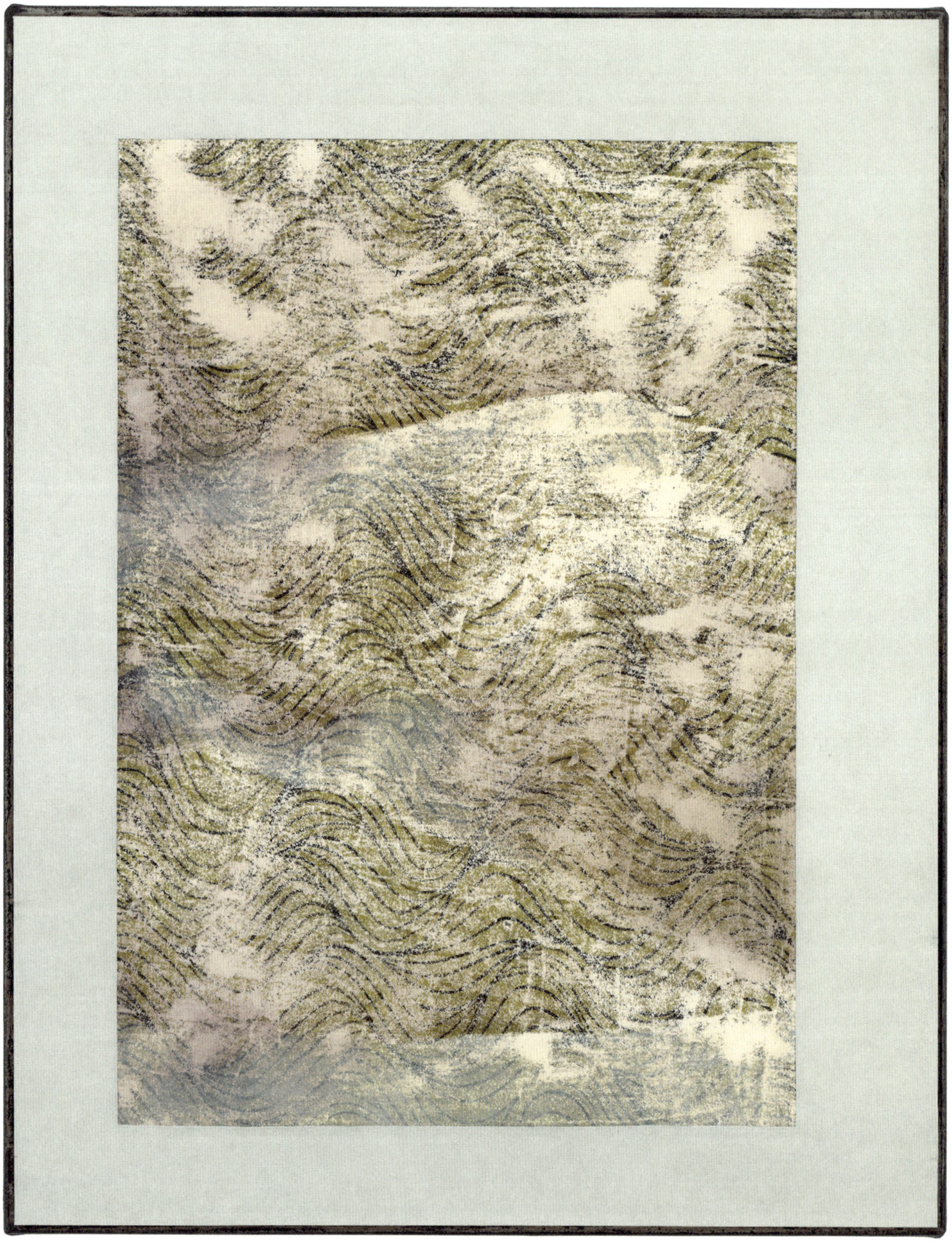

zange
cat. 1

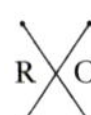

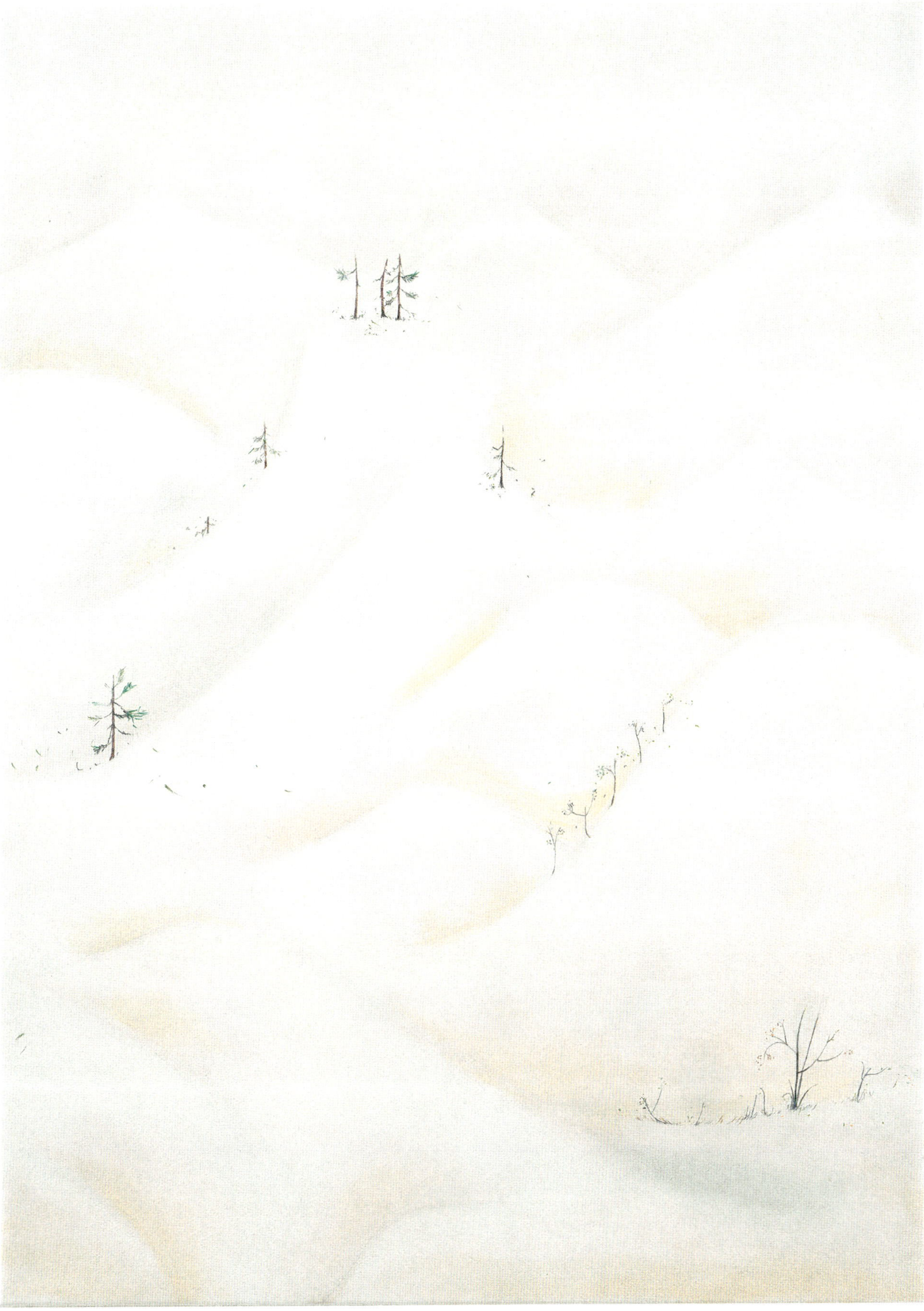

Inclinado
cat. 2

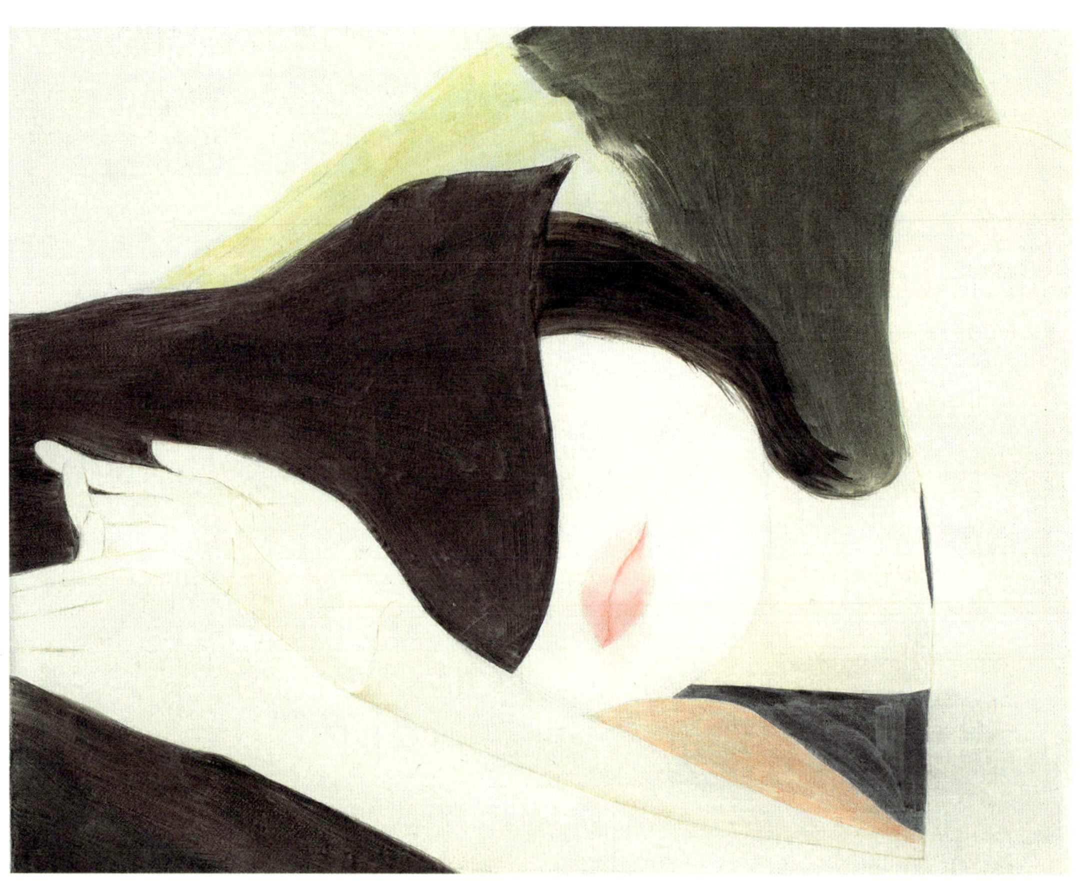

Tico-tico
cat. 3

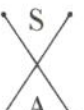

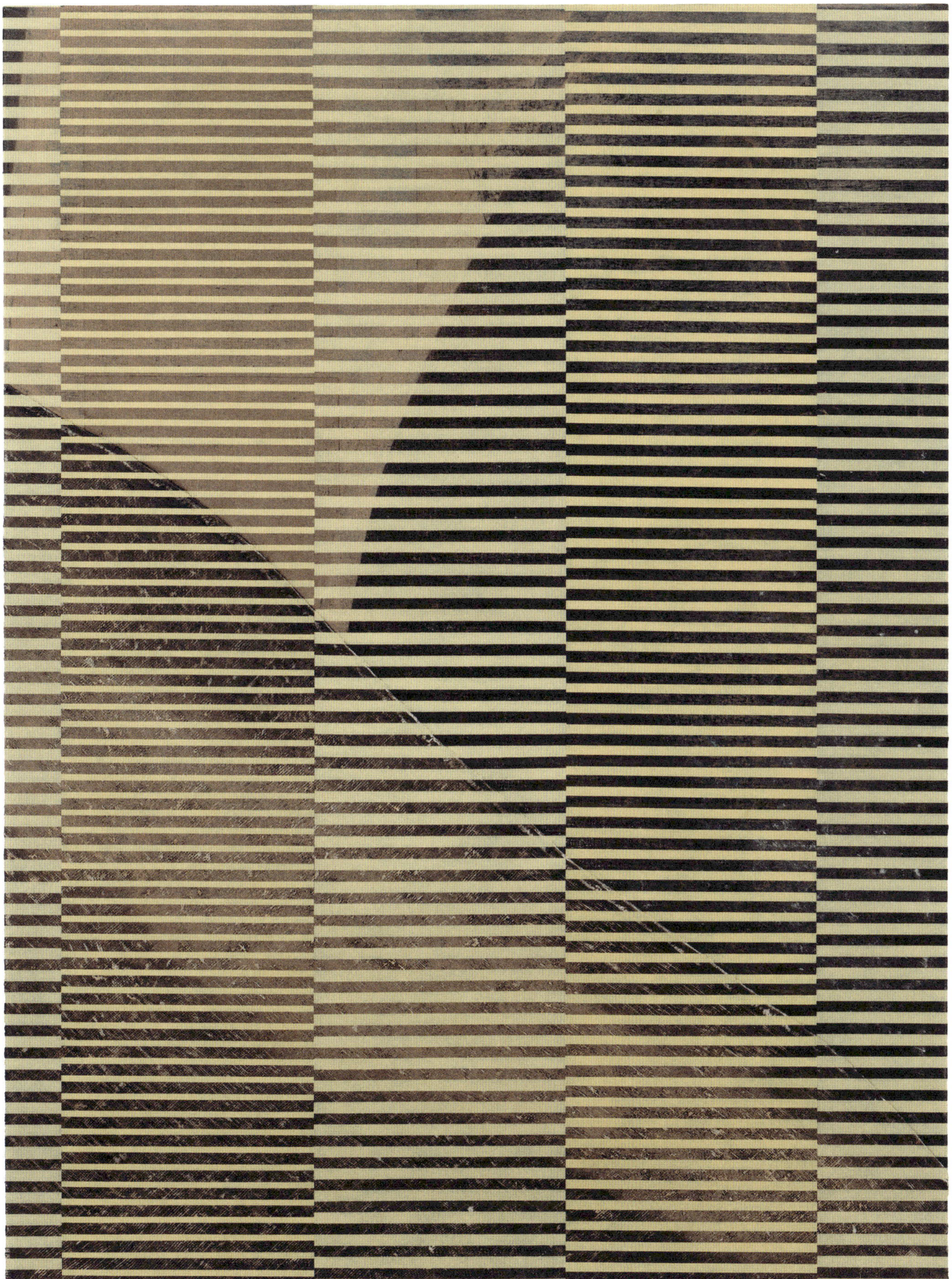

Stst (acea)

cat. 4

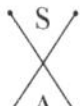

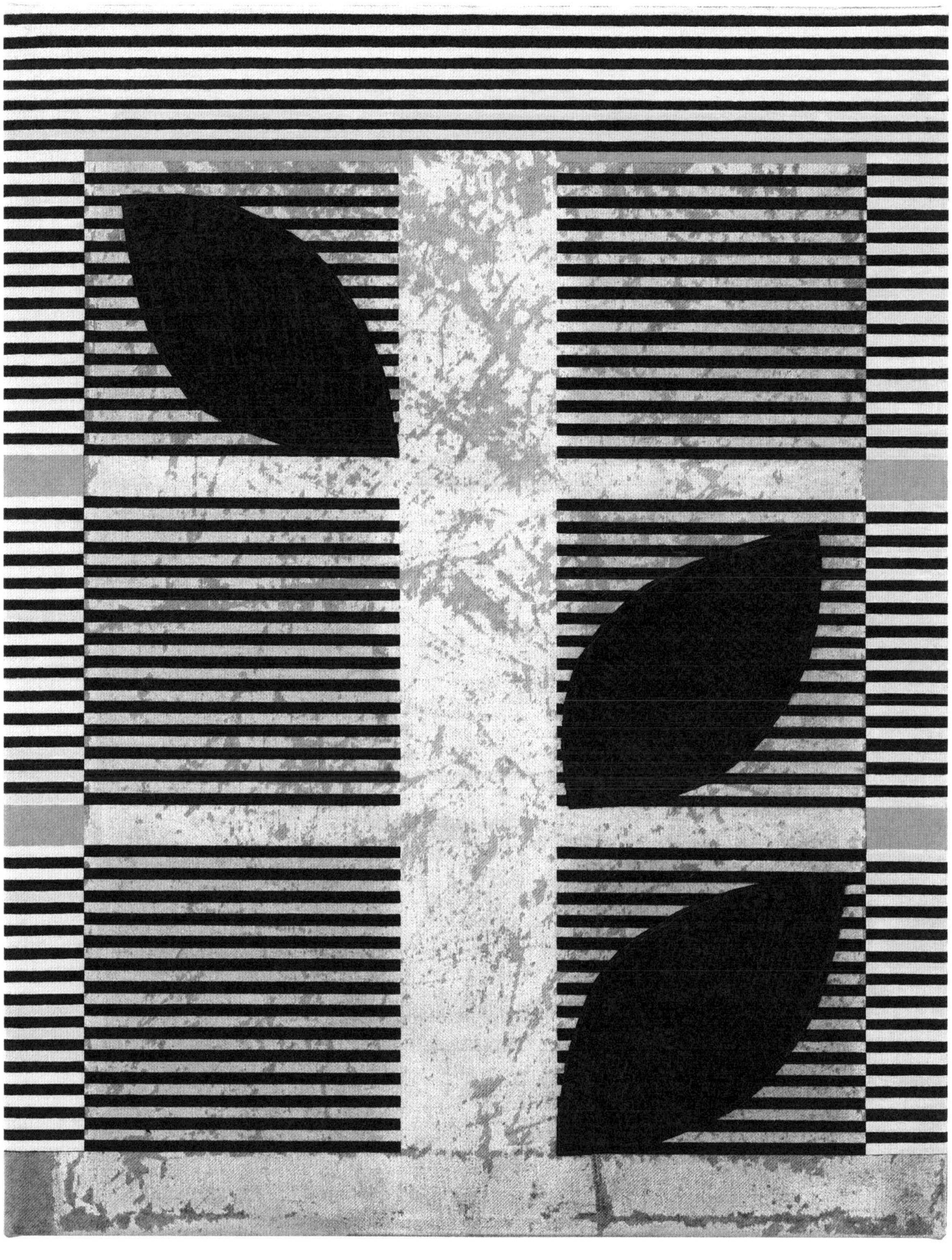

ior

cat. 5

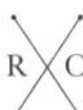

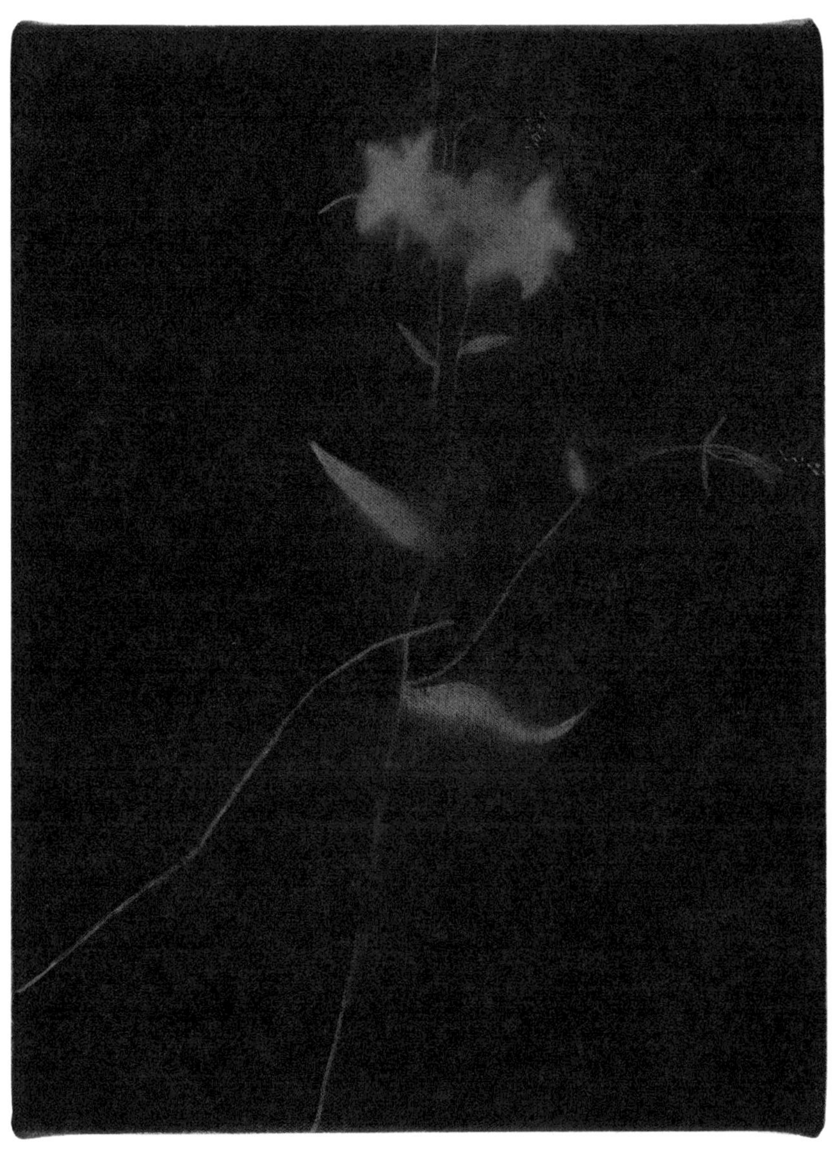

Silenzio
cat. 6

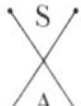

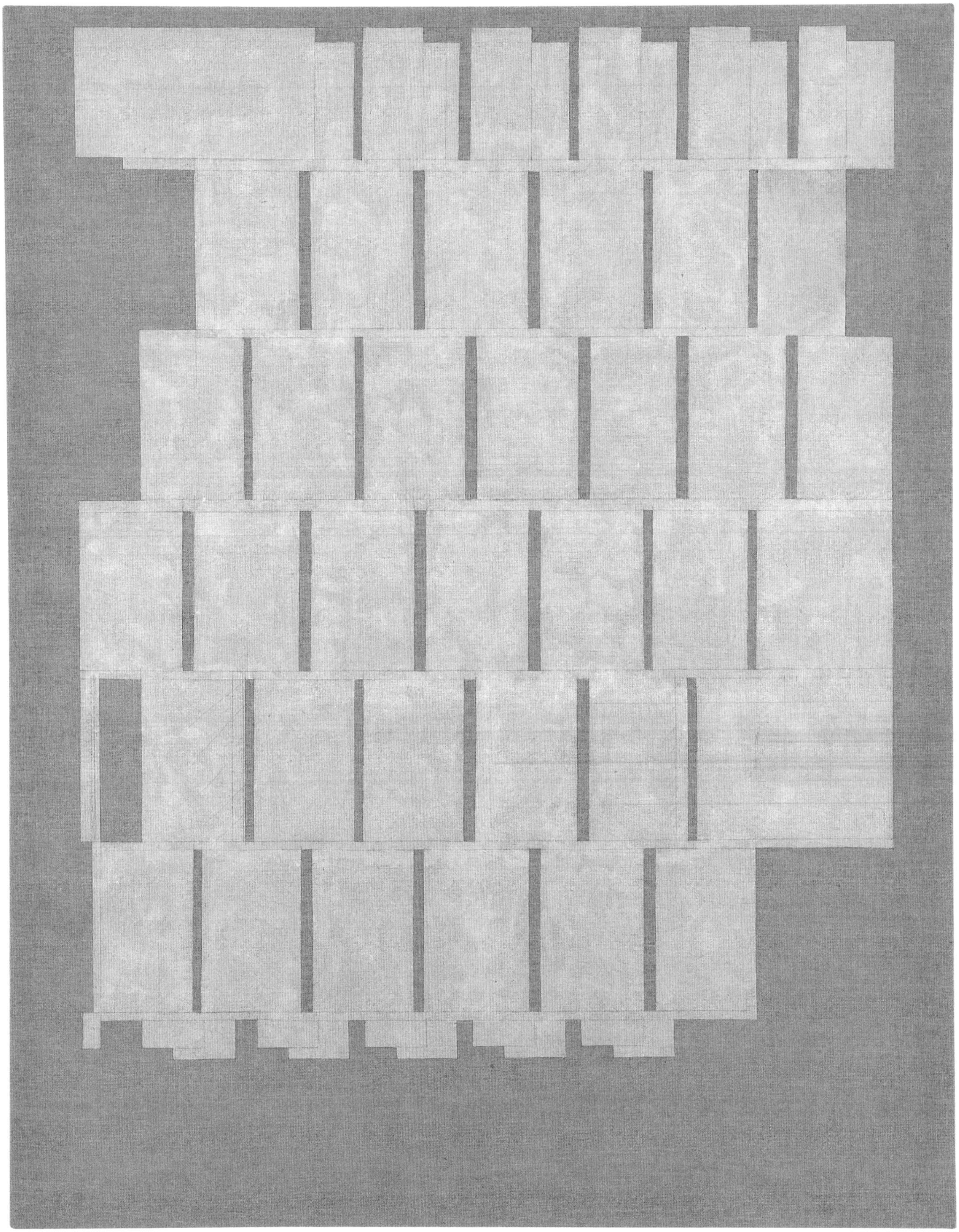

acco
cat. 7

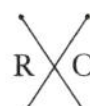

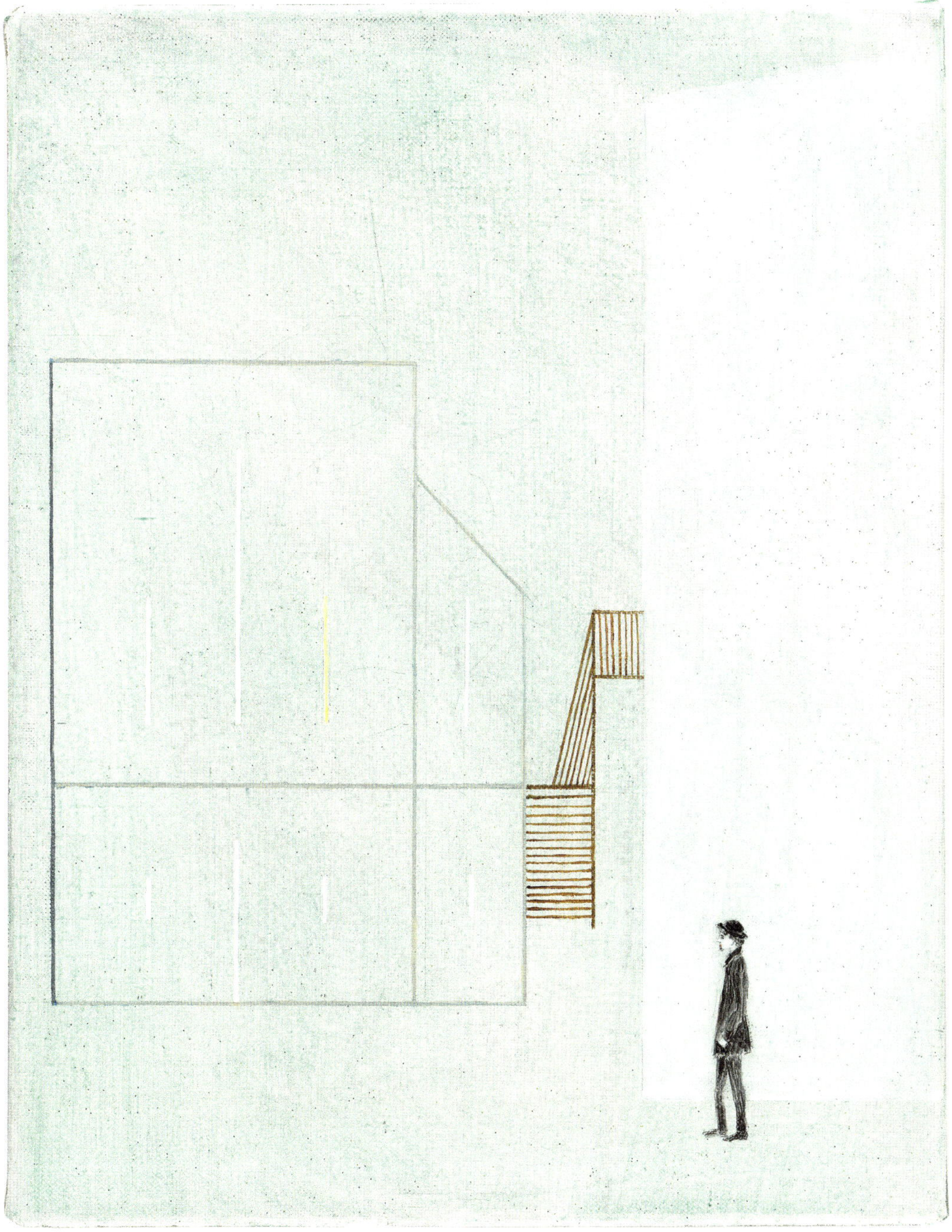

For you and for me

cat. 8

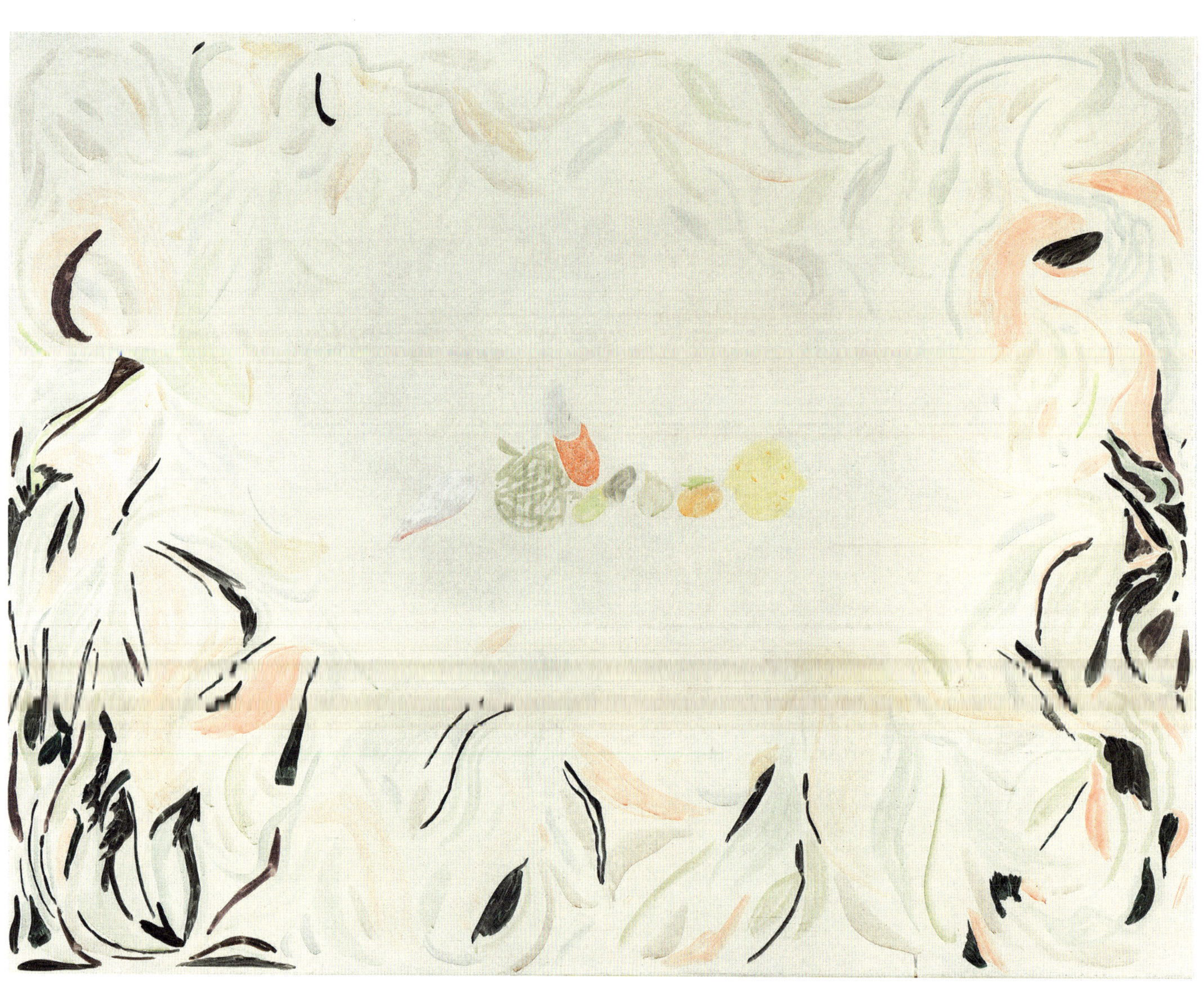

For Macunaíma
cat. 9

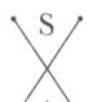

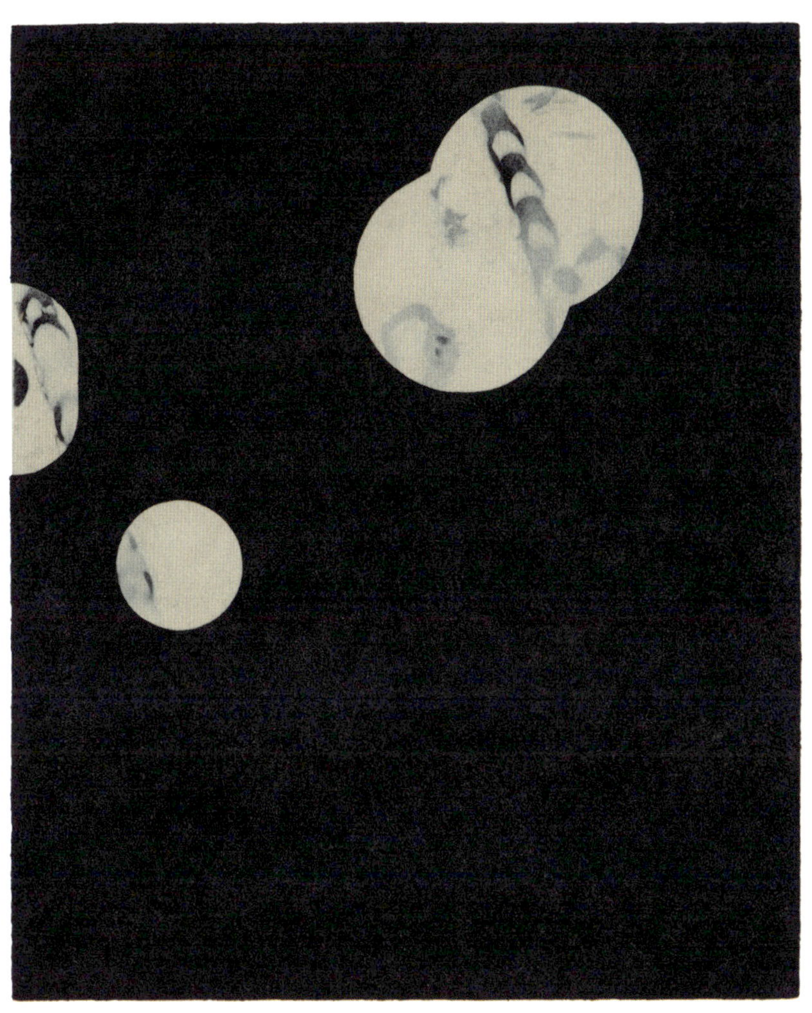

mounZ
cat. 10

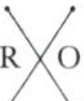

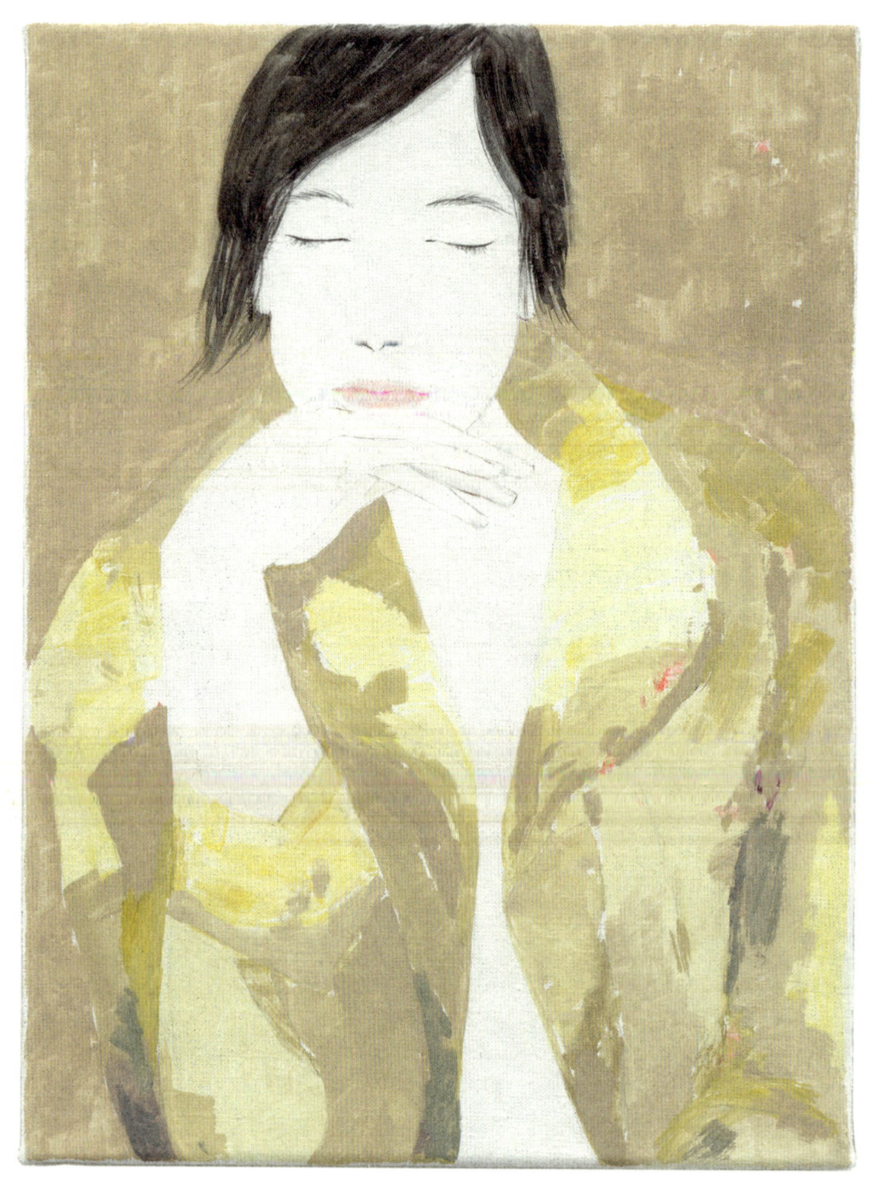

Esther
cat. 11

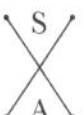

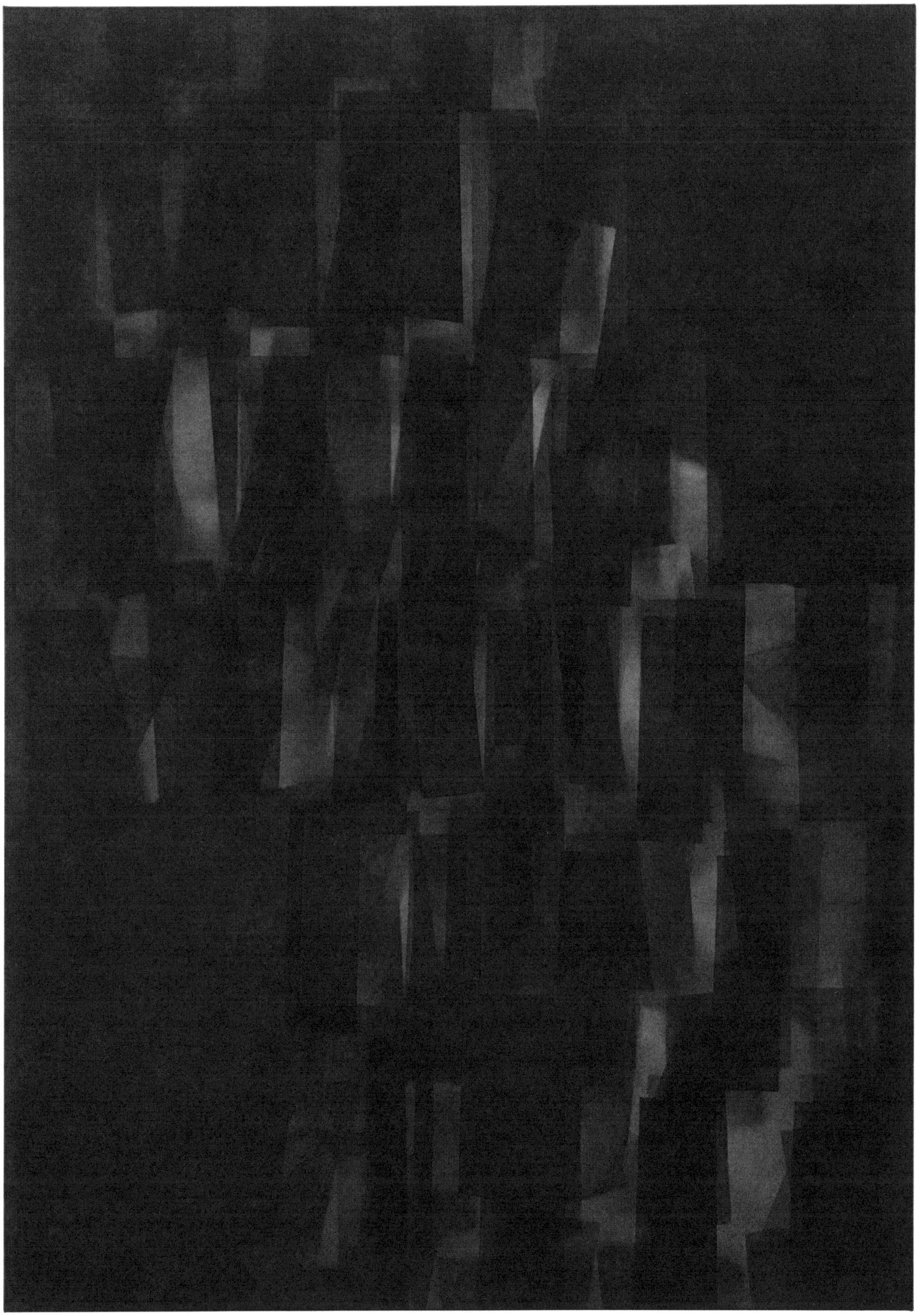

lioht
cat. 12

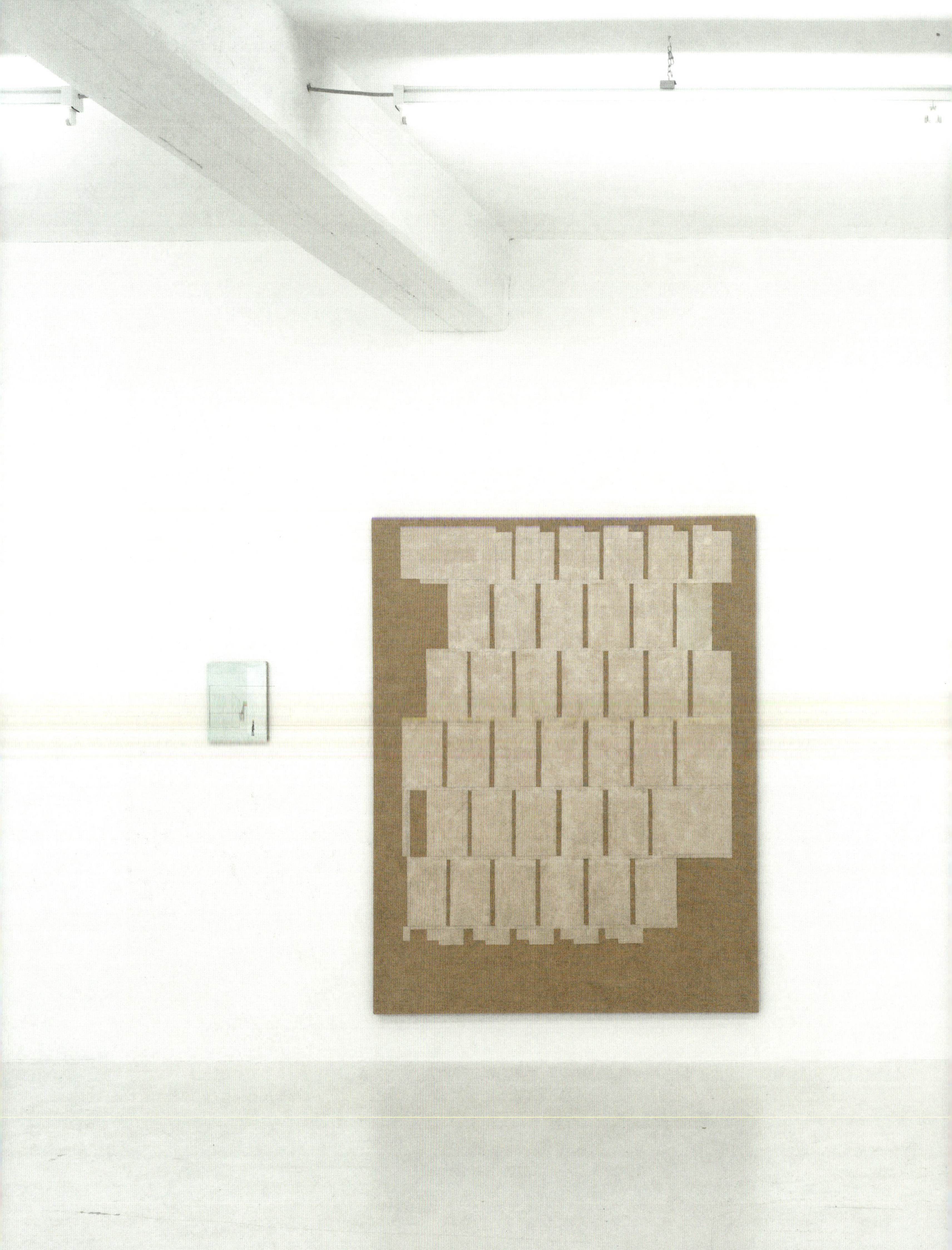

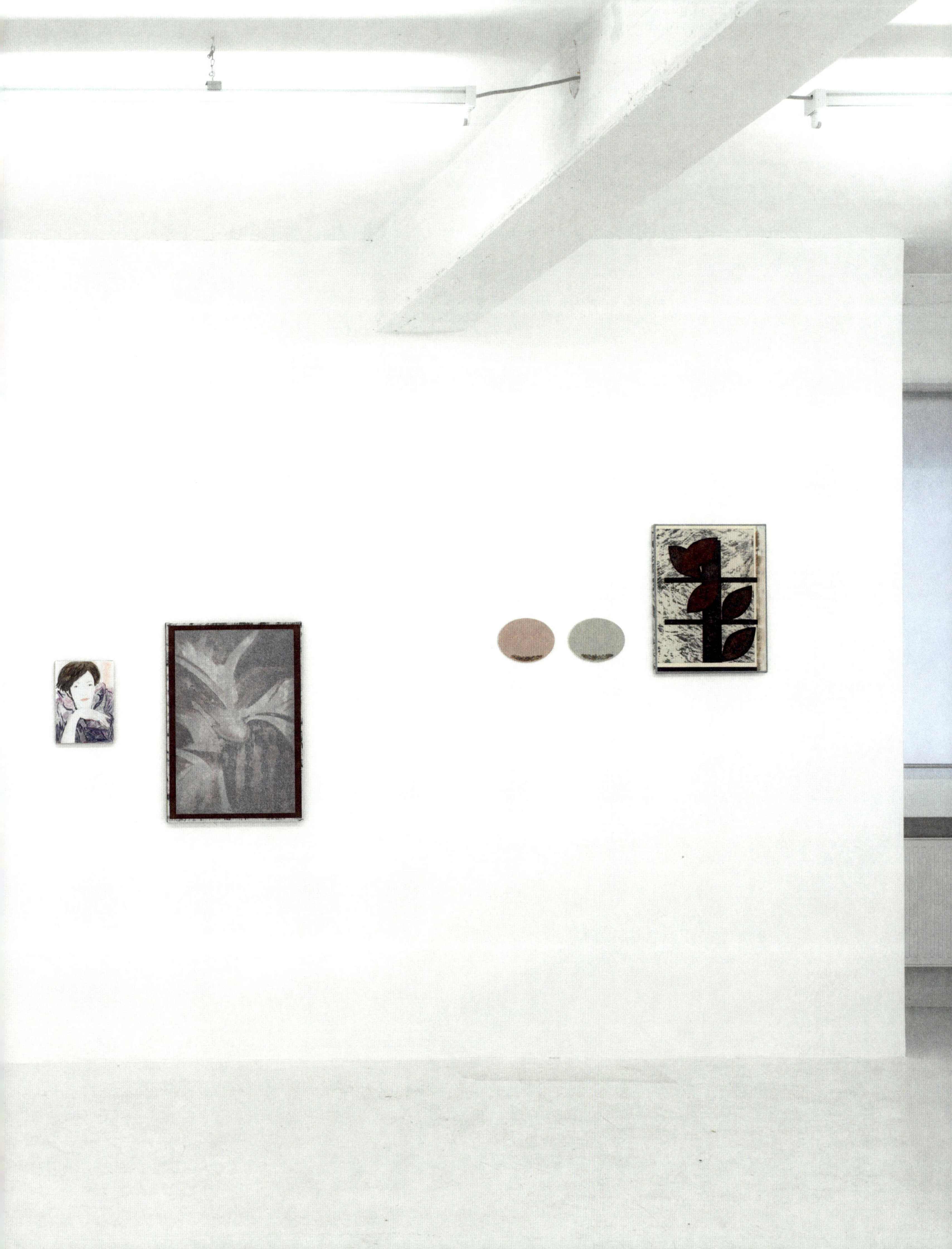

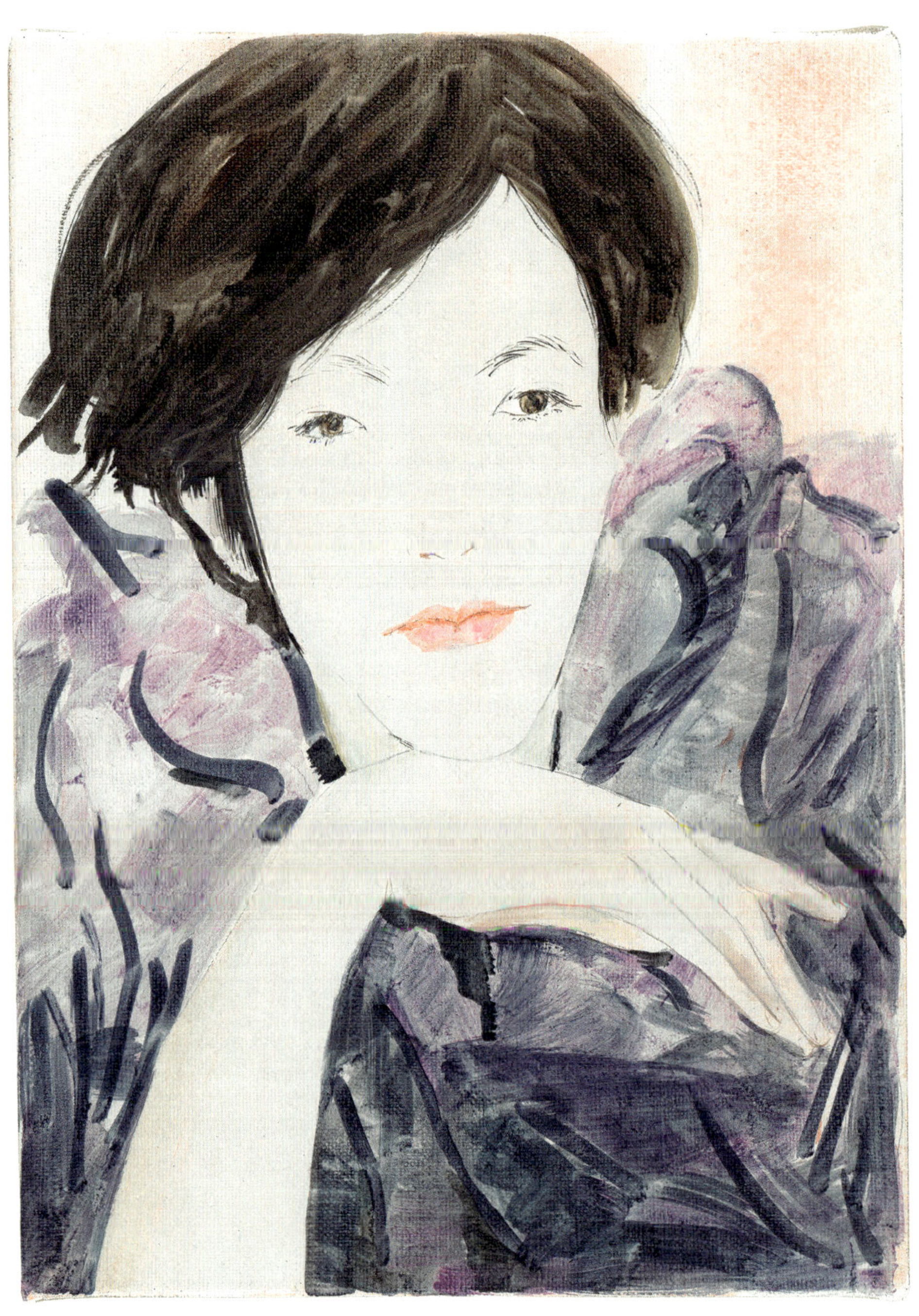

Seine erste Reise
cat. 13

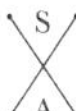

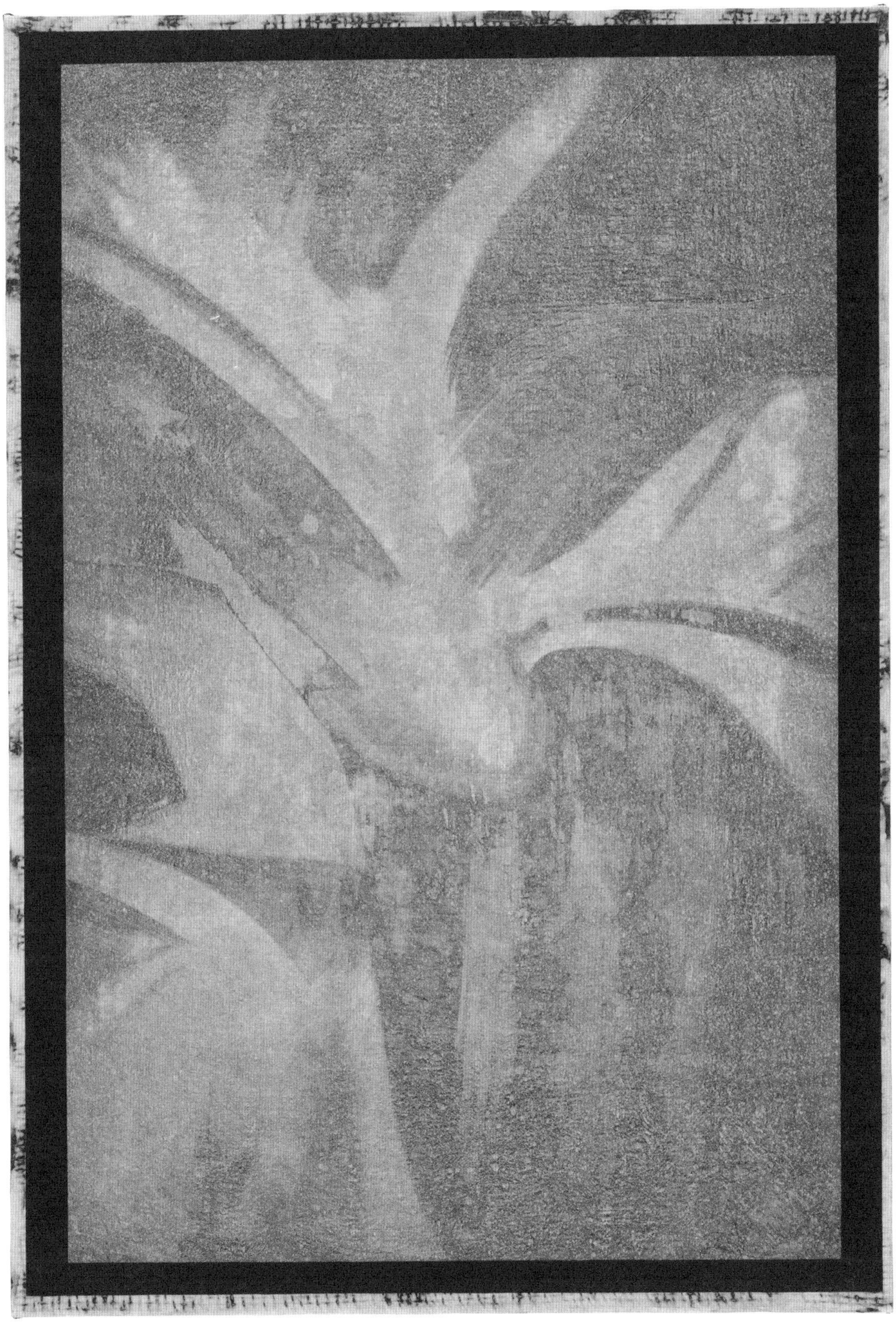

acea
cat. 14

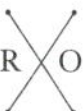

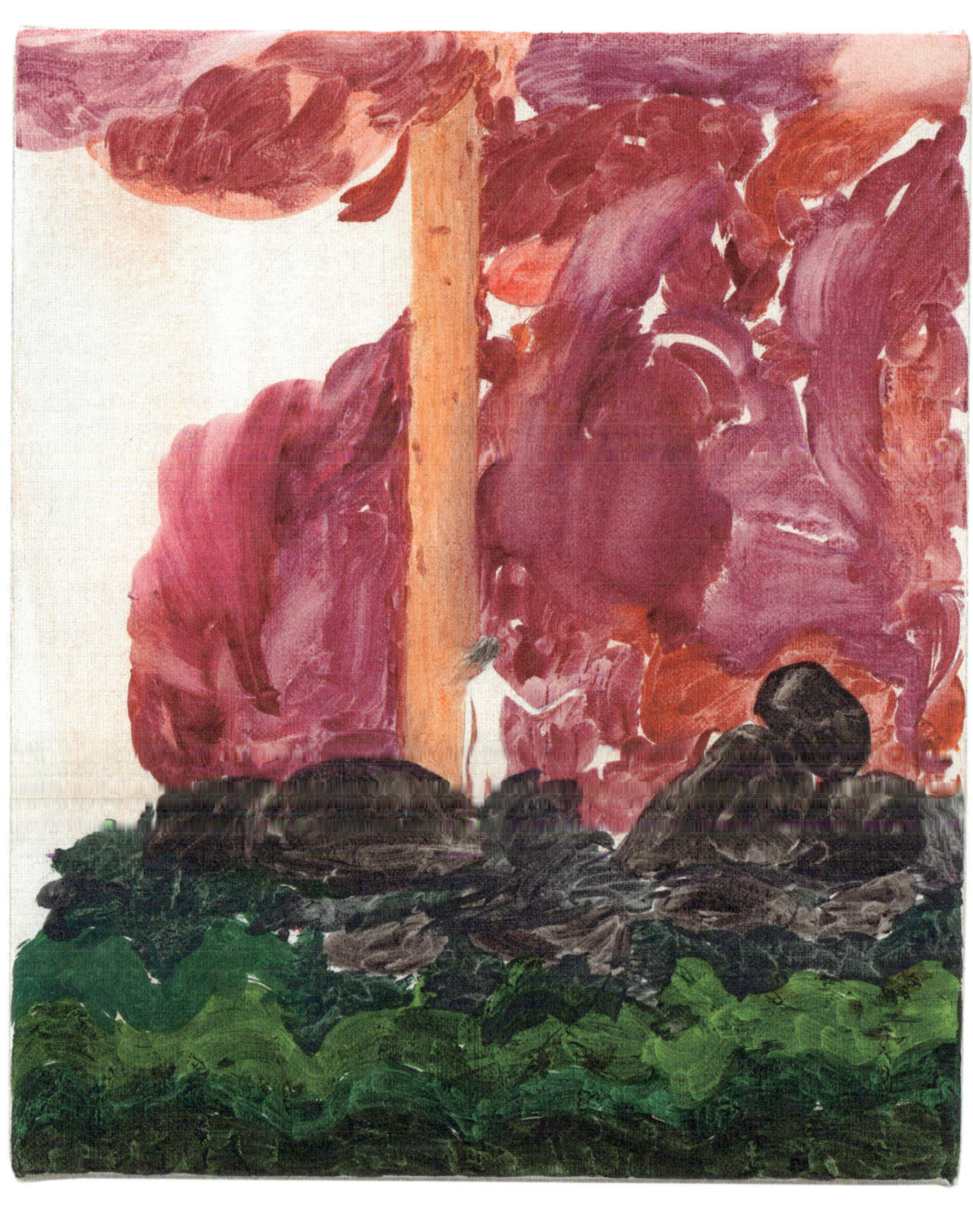

Touch
cat. 15

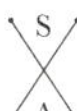

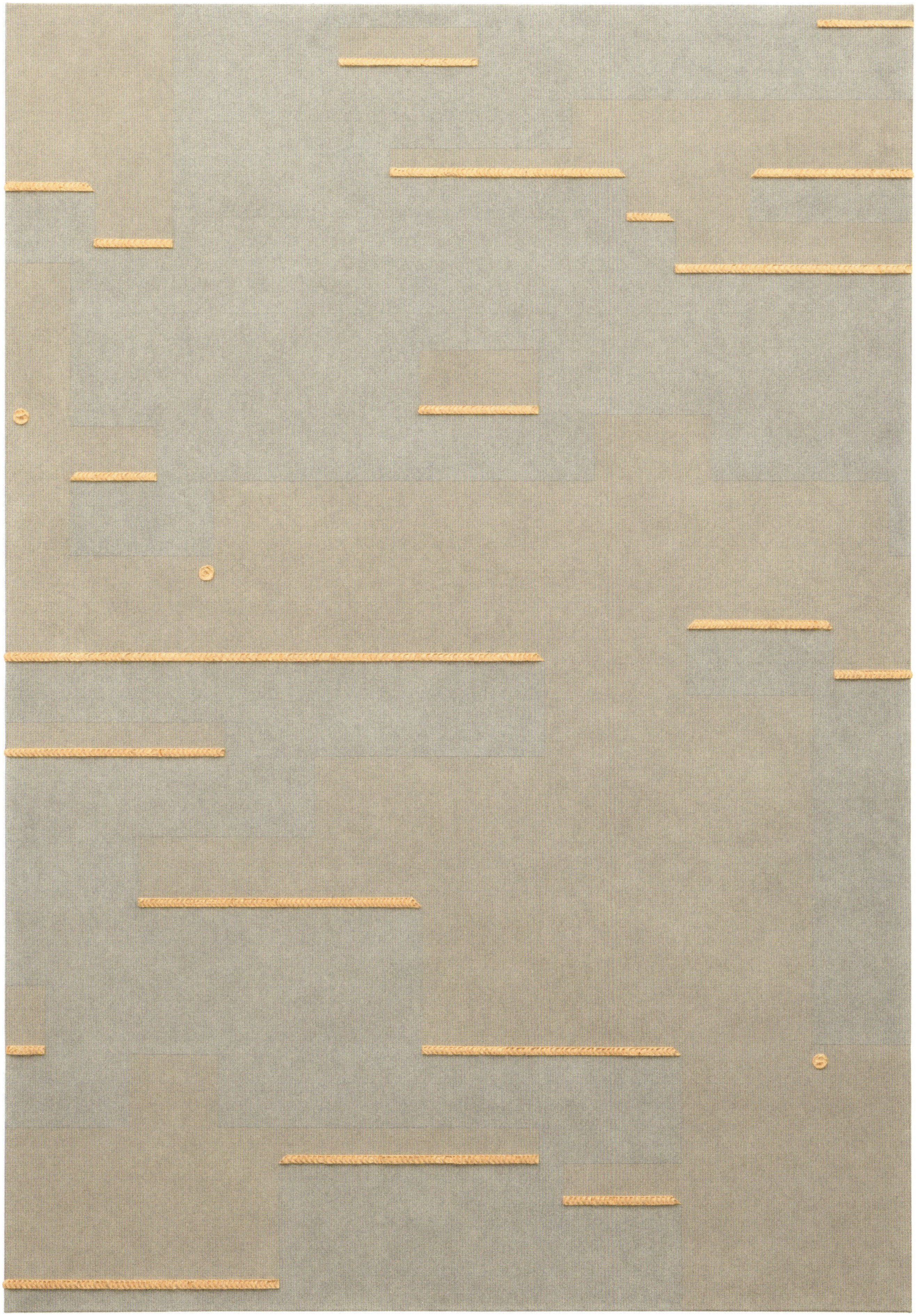

Zoa
cat. 16

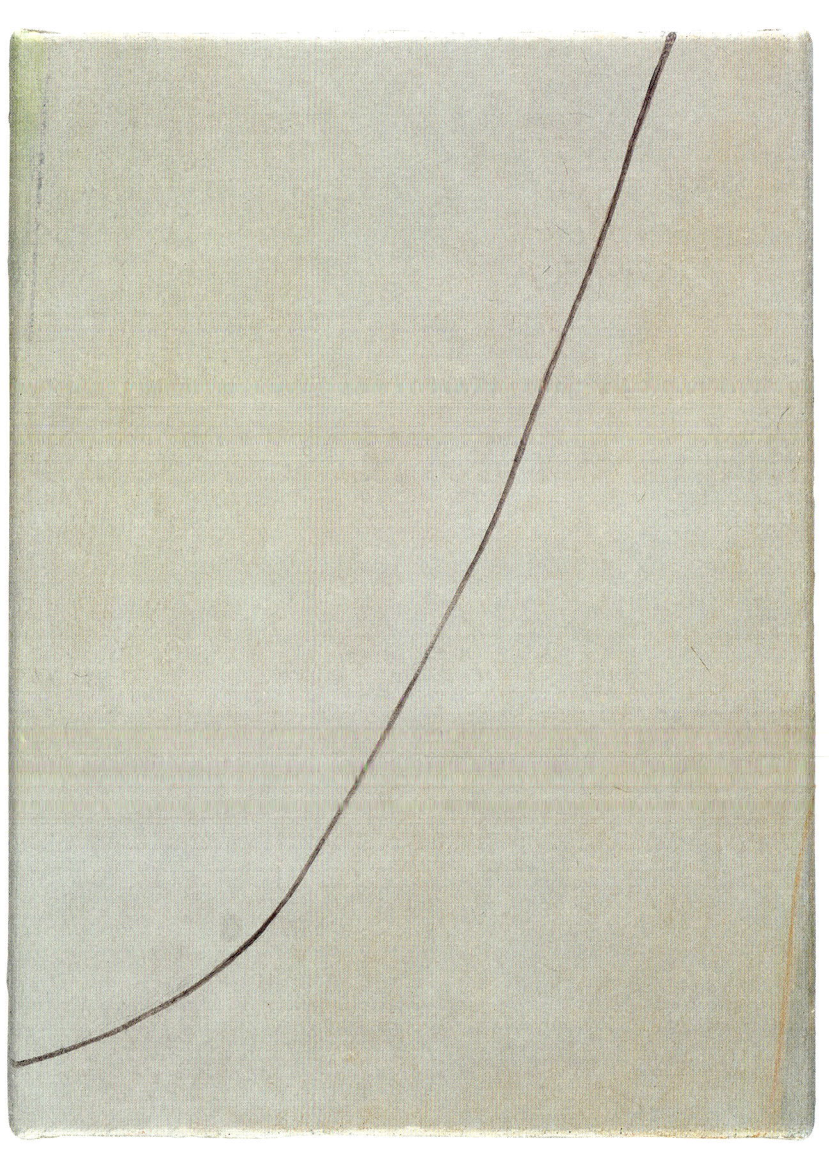

Das letzte Gespräch
cat. 17

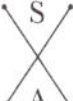

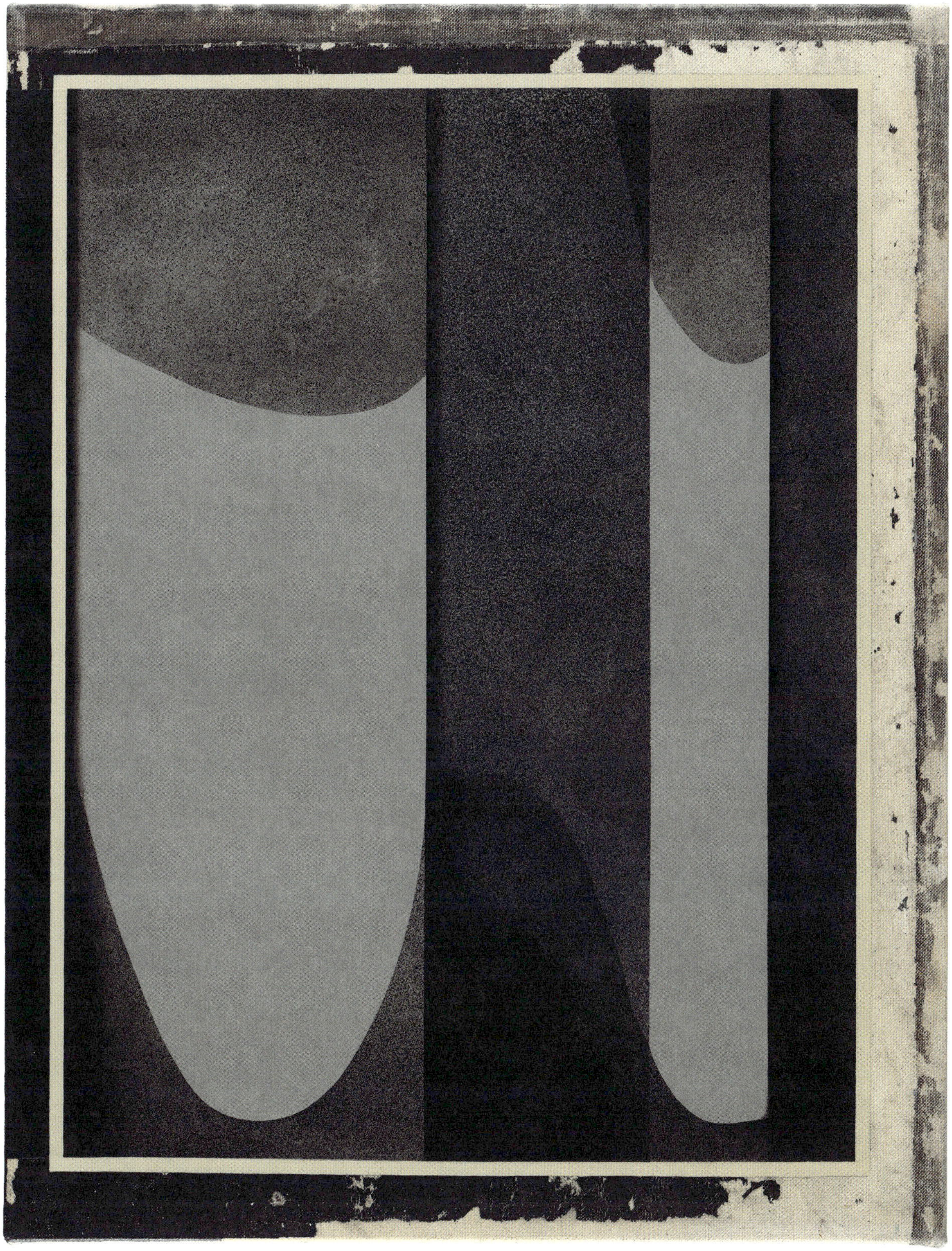

enwu

cat. 18

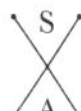

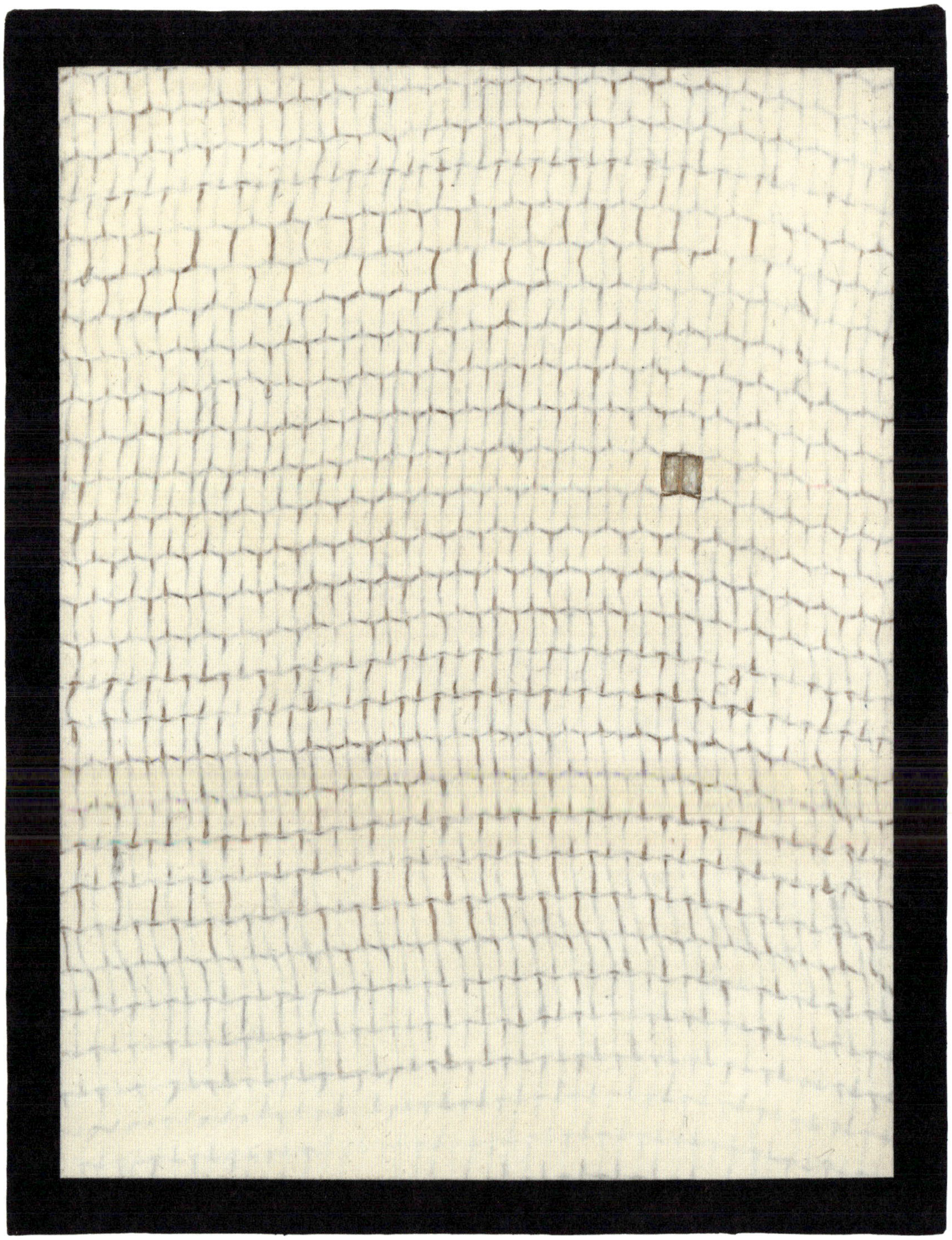

alop (FP)
cat. 19

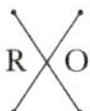

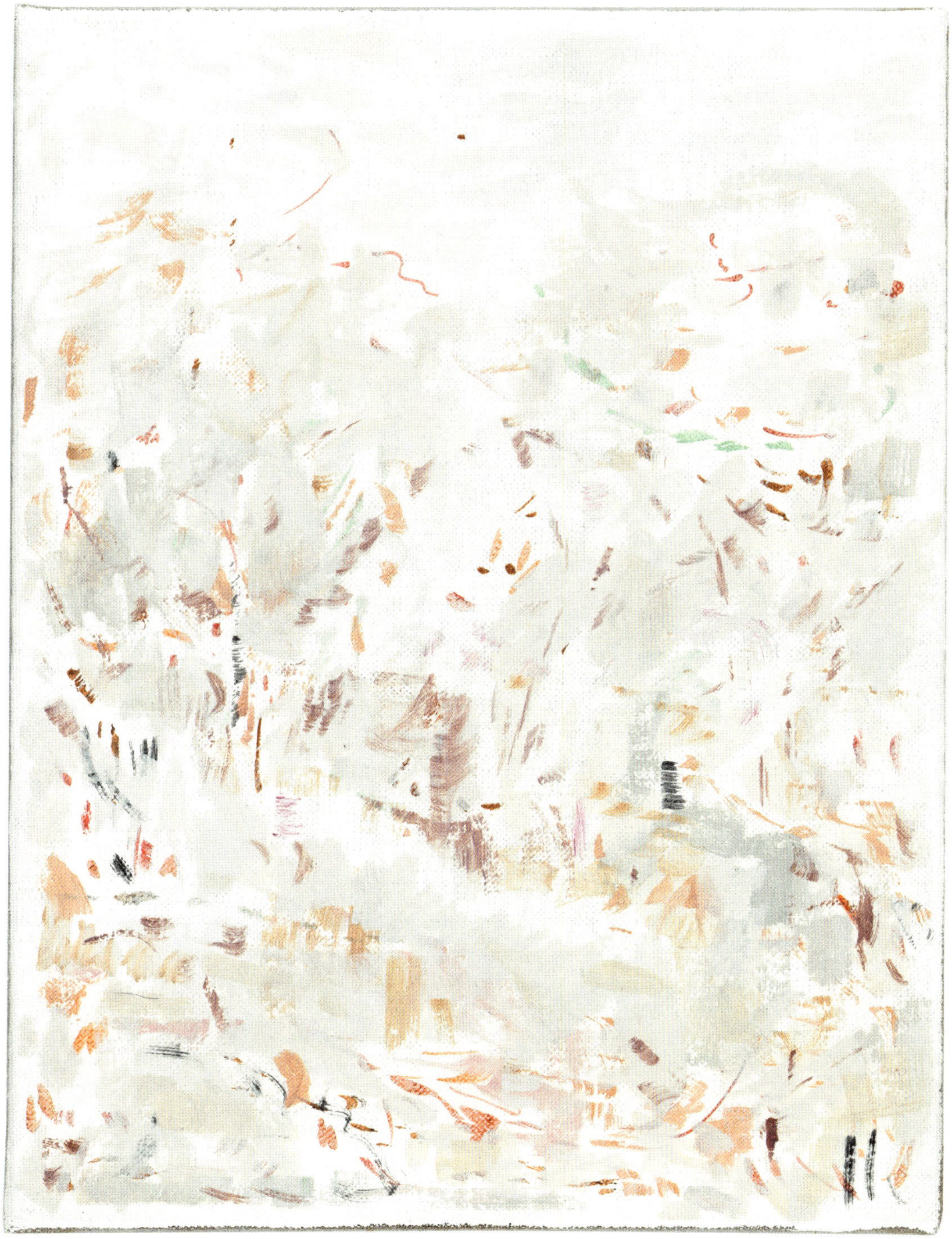

Eira
cat. 20

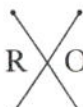

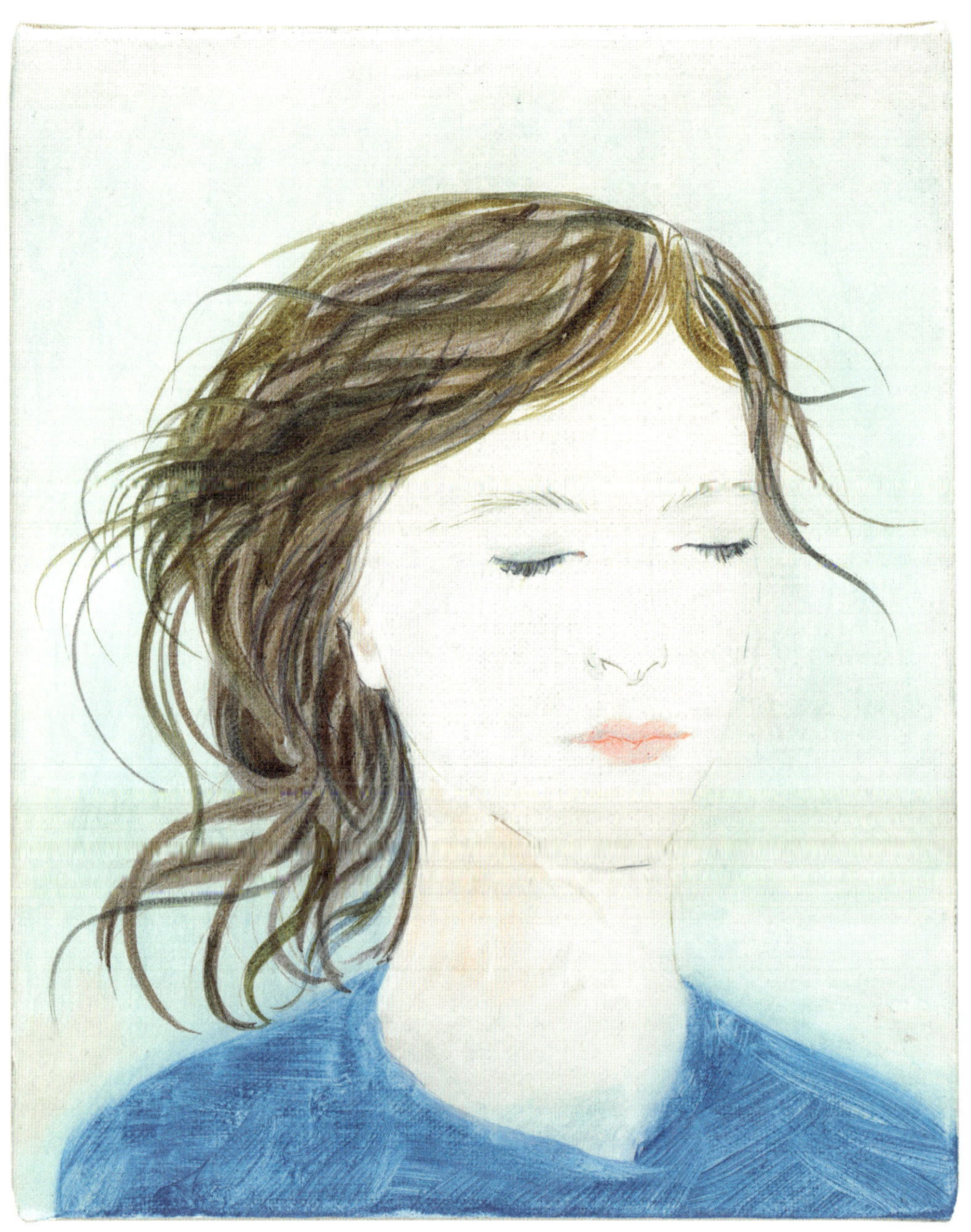

Credi
cat. 21

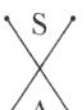

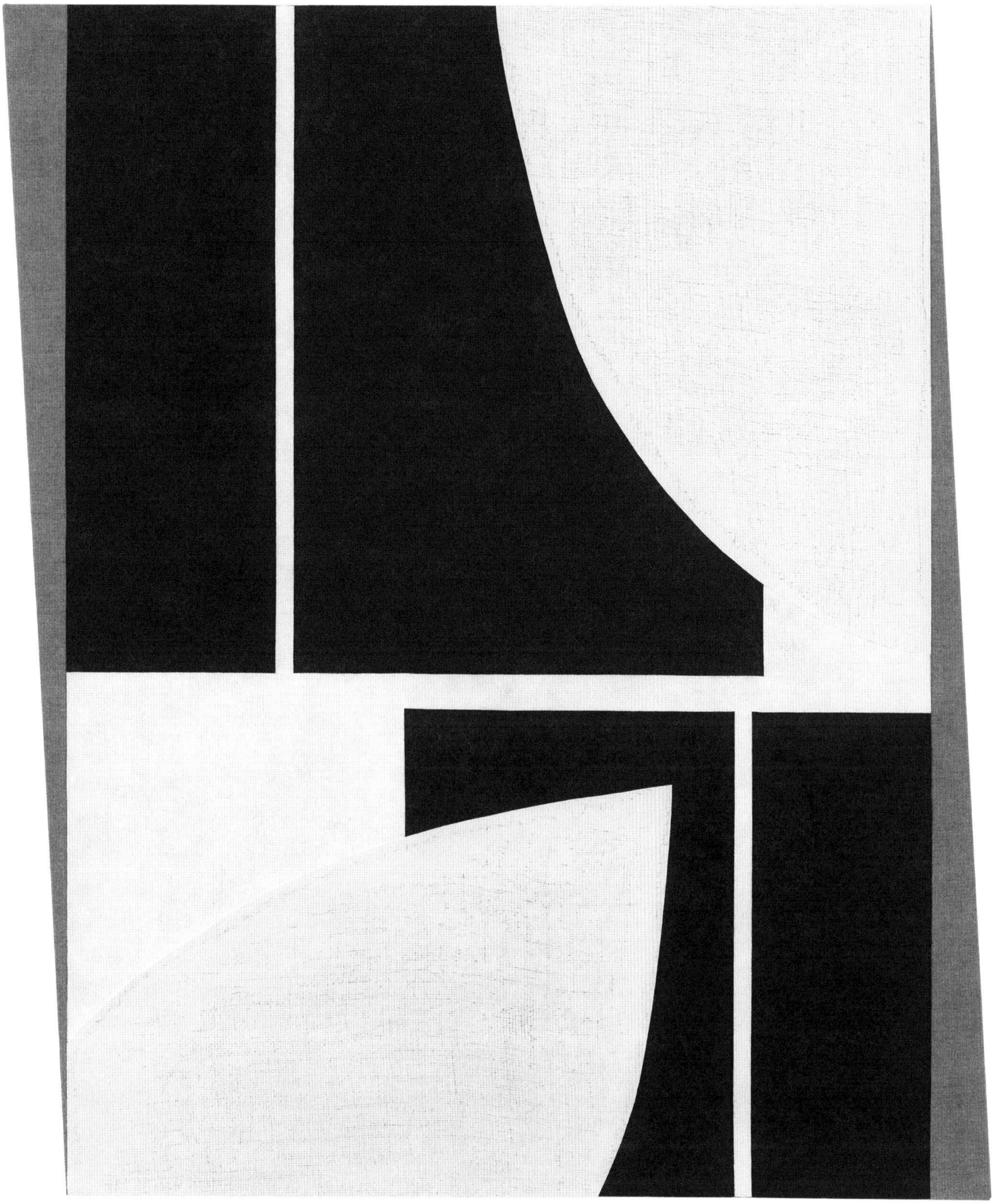

Cafor
cat. 22

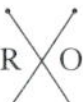

Zeitkapsel
cat. 23

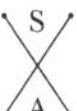

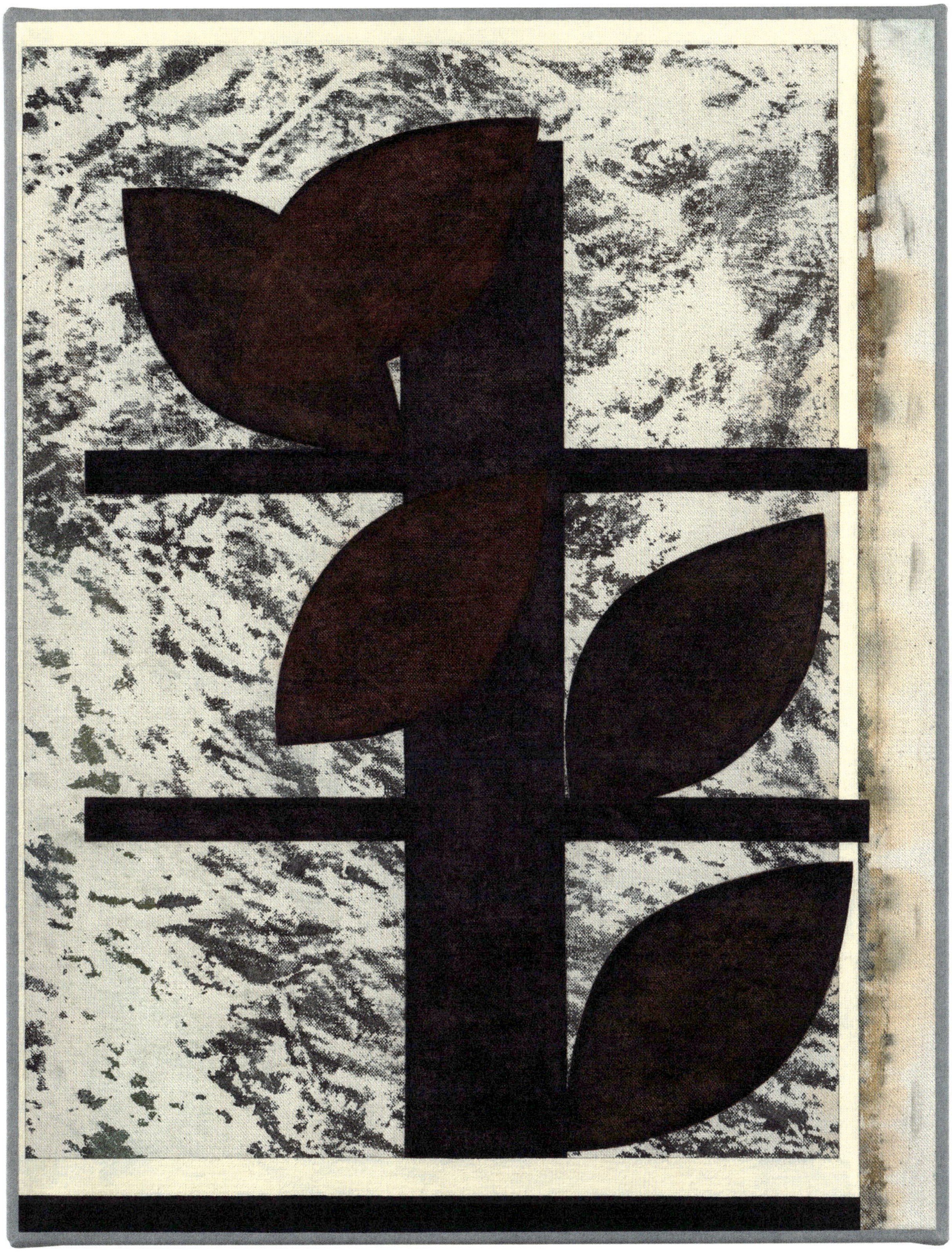

lauor

cat. 24

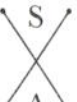

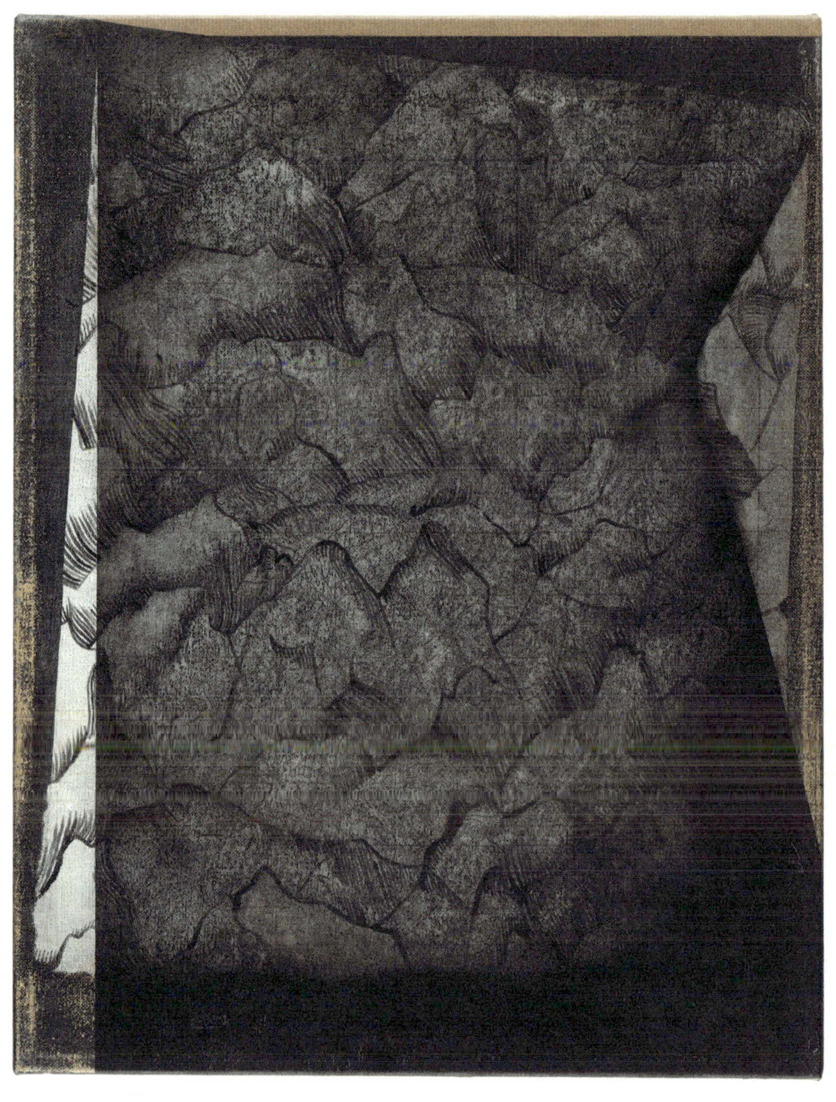

mons
cat. 25

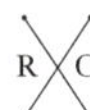

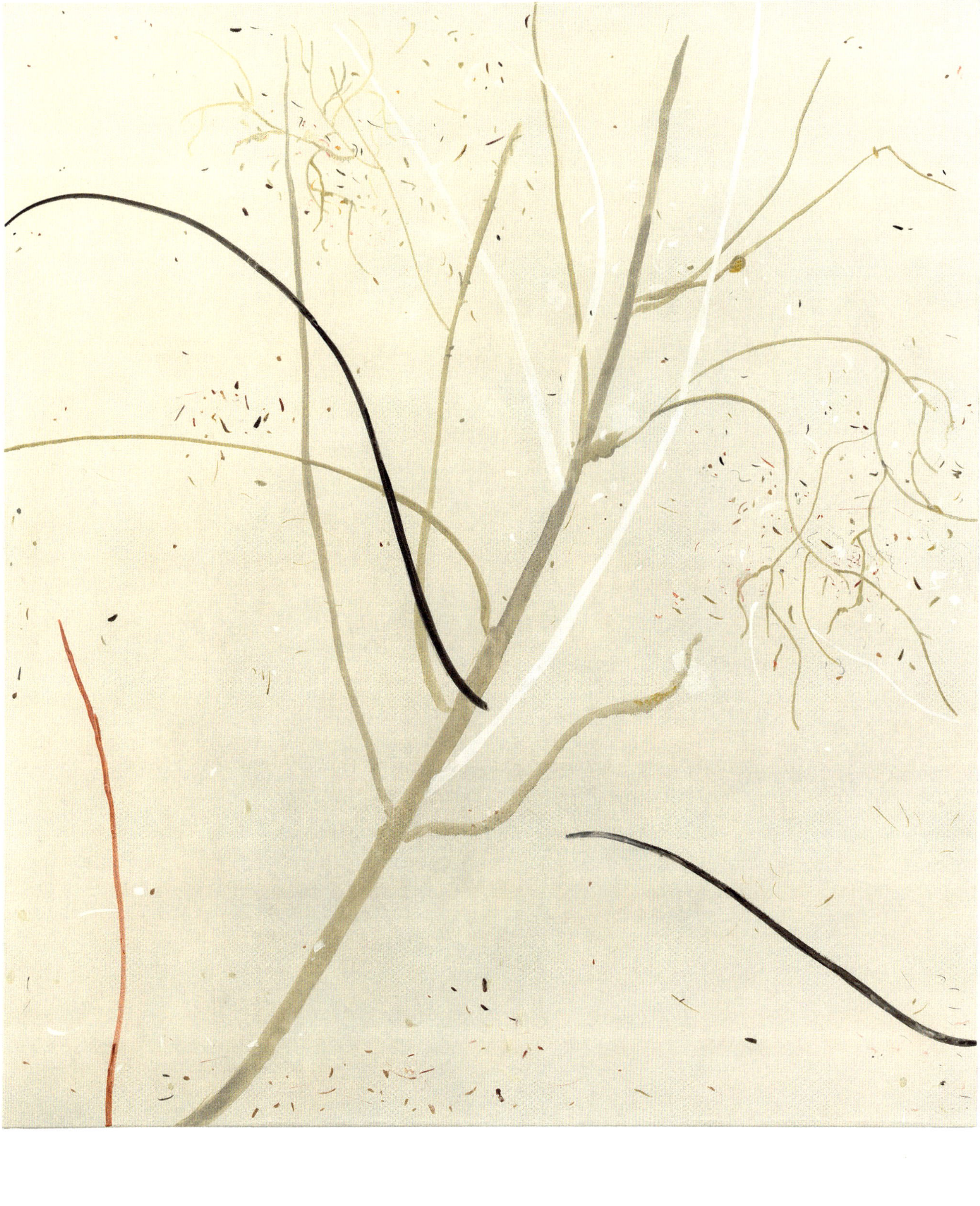

Chichia

cat. 26

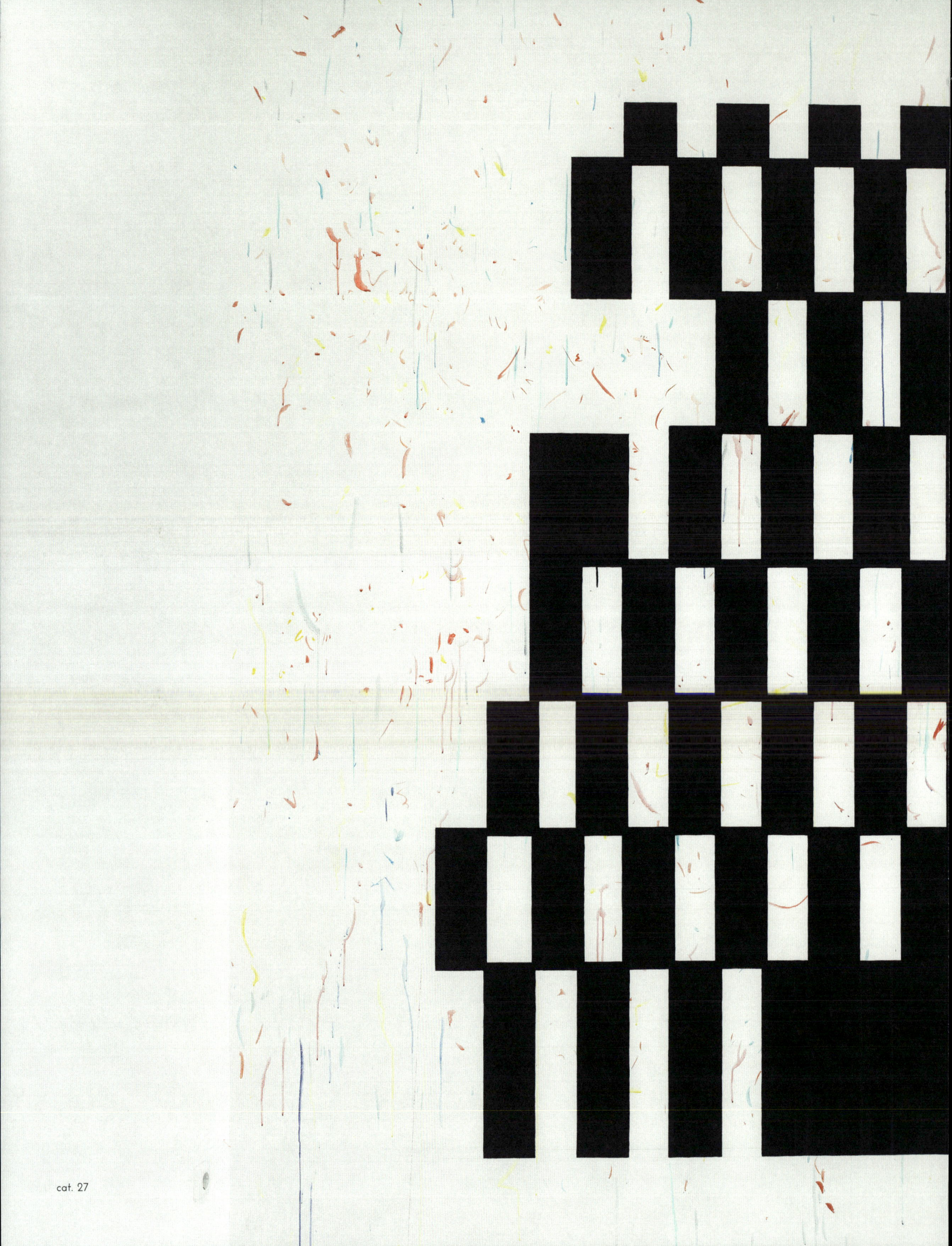

cat. 27

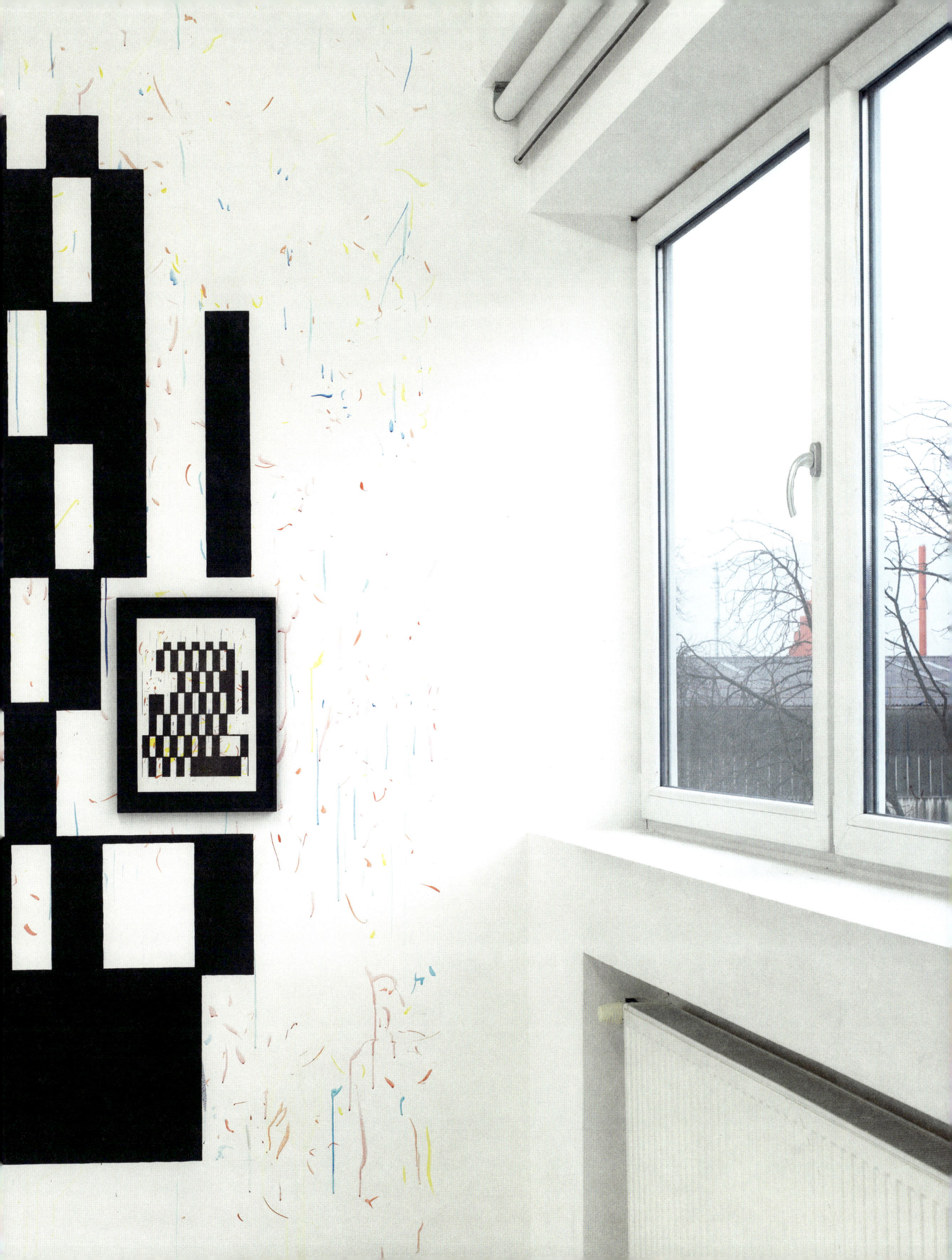

S
R O
A

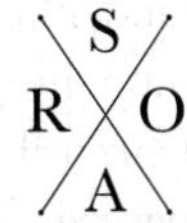

Rosilene Luduvico & Sabrina Fritsch

In der Ausstellung ROSA gehen die Künstlerinnen Sabrina Fritsch und Rosilene Luduvico in der Sammlung Philara eine temporäre Bindung ein und erkunden sowohl die Bedeutung einer Farbe als auch die „Legende einer Frau, die es nie gegeben hat“[1].

ROSA ist ein linguistischer und visueller Hybrid. Gleichwohl eine etymologische Zusammenführung der Anfangsbuchstaben der beiden Künstlerinnen, Rosilene und Sabrina, wie auch eine kritische Auseinandersetzung mit einer Farbe und ihrer Symbolik. Die Farbe Rosa entsteht aus einer Mischung von viel Weiß und wenig Rot. Semantisch steht das Farbadjektiv in einem historischen Kontext von Verfolgung und Emanzipation. Rosa Winkel dienten während des Nationalsozialismus dazu, Häftlinge zu kennzeichnen, die aufgrund ihrer Homosexualität inhaftiert worden waren. Seit den 1960er Jahren wird die Farbe Rosa im Kontext homosexueller Bewegungen oder umgangssprachlich in einer kommunistisch politischen Auslegung verwendet.[2] Gleichwohl markiert die Farblesart auch eine prototypische Stigmatisierung. Im Kontext von Kinderkleidung und Geschlechtszuschreibungen steht rosa in einer konzeptuellen Verbindung mit „Mädchen/Mädchenhaftigkeit“[3], die auch negativ als naiv bis zu spezifisch weiblich-dümmlich konnotiert sein kann.[4] In ROSA bemächtigen sich Rosilene Luduvico und Sabrina Fritsch dieser Farbe und stellen sich diesen Zuschreibungen entgegen.

Die abstrakten Arbeiten von Sabrina Fritsch changieren zwischen einer dominanten Gliederung, konkretem Farbauftrag und dispersiven Farbebenen. Das Leinwandformat dient dabei häufig als Rahmen für einen weitergedachten Logarithmus im Bildaufbau. Die Bildfläche wird in Segmente unterteilt, in deren Zwischenstucken durch Abschleifen oder Unbehandeltheit das Leinwandmaterial oder transparente Farbebenen sichtbar werden. Der durch Farbpräsenz und ihre Abwesenheit erzeugte Dualismus evoziert gleichzeitig den Eindruck von Zugang und Unzugänglichkeit. In *Stst (acea)* von 2013 vollzieht sich dieser deutlich. Eine asynchrone Lamellenwand überlagert die angeschliffene, diffuse rückgelagerte Ebene. Es entsteht eine modern tektonische Form der Verschleierung, die trotz ihrer Geradlinigkeit von Sinnlichkeit zeugt. Diese systematische Konfiguration erzeugt ein Flimmern und erschwert das Durchdringen zur zweiten Ebene. Konträr dazu basieren die Arbeiten von Rosilene Luduvico auf Schwüngen, floralen Ausformungen und sanften Strichen in Pastellfarben. Gerne folgt man der Verspieltheit ihres zarten Duktus. In *Credi* und *Chichia* evoziert Luduvico Sonntagsgefühle: das Rascheln von Baumkronen, der Wind in den Haaren, das Gewahrwerden von Sekunden. Ihre anmutigen Porträts wie *Seine erste Reise* nähern sich dem menschlichen Antlitz feinfühlig. Malerisch streichelnd erfassen sie die Aura einer Person oder eines Moments.

Dialektisch begegnen sich die Positionen von Luduvico und Fritsch als vermeintlich künstlerisches Komplement. Zu Paaren gehangen werden die Arbeiten von Fritsch und Luduvico einander gegenübergestellt. Indes treten sie besonders durch ihre formale Differenz in eine wechselseitige Beziehung, die eine neue Konnotation beider Arbeiten ermöglicht. Dabei werden die charakteristischen Züge einer künstlerischen Position in der jeweils anderen betont. Plötzlich werden die geometrischen Formen aus Luduvicos Arbeiten sowie die Zärtlichkeiten aus Fritschs Arbeiten akzentuierter – als Duell erwartet, tritt diese Paarung als Duett hervor. Ohne die Eigenständigkeit der jeweiligen Arbeit zu mindern, entfaltet sich eine neue Erzähl- oder Bedeutungsdiversität. Durch *acea* (Fritsch) meint man die Stofflichkeit der Bluse in *Seine erste Reise* (Luduvico) zu erfassen. Die segmentierte Aufteilung in *acco* (Fritsch) potenziert den architektonischen Aufbau in *For you and for me* (Luduvico). Unter Beibehaltung von Abstraktion entstehen durch diese Paarungen aphoristische Narrationen.

Was als Dialektik konzipiert wird, entpuppt sich als visuelle Synthese. Gesteigert wird diese finale Verschmelzung in *ROSA*, einer gemeinschaftlichen Wandarbeit, die in den Räumen der Sammlung Philara realisiert wurde. Geschmeidige Striche in abgeschwächten Primärfarben, die sich tänzelnd über die Wand ziehen, werden von radikalen schwarzen Rastern überlagert.
ROSA ist die Frau vieler Nuancen. Der kuratorische Dualismus wird hier methodisch ins Bild übertragen und somit zur Synthese. ROSA ist gleichermaßen bestimmt und zärtlich sowohl präsent und abwesend. Fern von naiv und dümmlich ist ROSA wohlkalkuliert und empfindsam konzipiert.
ROSA ist kein Prototyp.
Nicht rosa, sondern eine Wechselgestalt, die viele Personen in einer Person sein kann.

1 Bachmann, Ingeborg: *Malina*, Frankfurt am Main 1980, S. 61.

2 Caroline Kaufmann, *Zur Semantik der Farbadjektive rosa, pink und rot*, München 2006, S. 35.

3 Ebd. S. 74.

4 Ebd. S. 67.

In the exhibition ROSA, the artists Sabrina Fritsch and Rosilene Luduvico team up for a temporary project in the Philara Collection; and they explore both the significance of a colour as well as the "legend of a woman who never existed."[1]

ROSA is a linguistic and visual hybrid. It is also an etymological fusion of the initial letters of the artists' names, Rosilene and Sabrina, as well as a critical exploration of a colour and its symbolism. The colour pink is created by mixing mainly white with a hint of red. Semantically, the colour adjective is located within a historical setting of persecution and emancipation. The National Socialists used pink triangles to indicate that certain men got imprisoned because of their homosexuality. Since the 1960s the colour pink has been adopted in the context of homosexual movements, or colloquially as a communist political version.[2] Nevertheless, interpreting the colour also marks a prototypical stigmatization. In terms of children's clothing and gender attributions, pink is associated with the idea of "girl/girlishness"[3] that can also have a negative connotation as naïve to specifically feminine and insipid.[4] In ROSA, Rosilene Luduvico and Sabrina Fritsch take over this colour and adopt counter-positions to these connotations.

The abstract works by Sabrina Fritsch alternate between a dominant structure, concrete application of colour and dispersive colour layers. The canvas format often serves in this process as a frame for further elaboration on a logarithm in the picture composition. The picture surface is subdivided into segments with transitional sections where the canvas material or transparent colour layers are visibly exposed by sandpapering or by being unfinished. The dualism of the colour application created by its presence and absence simultaneously evokes the impression of access and inaccessibility. This is evidently accomplished in the 2013 *Stst (acea)*. An asynchronous wall of lamello slats overlaps the sanded, diffuse recessed layer. A modern tectonic form of obscuring is created that evokes sensuality despite its linearity. This systematic configuration produces a flickering effect and makes it more difficult to see through to the second layer.
In contrast, the works by Rosilene Luduvico are based on sweeping flows, floral shapes and gentle lines in pastel colours. It is a pleasure to follow the playfulness of her delicate flowing style. In *Credi* and *Chichia,* Luduvico evokes Sunday feelings: the rustling of treetops, the wind in one's hair and becoming aware of seconds. Her graceful portraits such as *Seine erste Reise* sensitively focus on the human face. With painterly caresses they capture the aura of a person or a moment.

The positions of Luduvico and Fritsch meet dialectically as a presumed artistic complement. The works by Fritsch and Luduvico are displayed in pairs and juxtaposed. In particular, however, due to their formal difference they establish a reciprocal relationship that makes possible a new connotation for both works. The characteristic traits of an artistic position are therefore emphasized in the respective other. Suddenly, the geometric forms of Luduvico's works as well as the endearing aspects of Fritsch's compositions become more accentuated – this pairing is anticipated as a duel and appears as a duet.
Without diminishing the originality of the respective work, a new diversity emerges of narrative or meaning. In viewing *acea* (Fritsch), one has the impression of capturing the materiality of the blouse in *Seine erste Reise* (Luduvico). The segmented sub-divisions in *acco* (Fritsch) are raised to the power of the architectural composition in *For you and for me* (Luduvico). These pairings form aphoristic narrations by retaining abstraction. What is devised as a dialectic turns out to be visual synthesis.

This final fusing together is heightened in *ROSA*, a collaborative wall mural, which was realised in the exhibition room of the Philara Collection. Smooth strokes in toned-down primary colours, which move, dancing, across the wall, have radical black grid patterns superimposed on them.
ROSA is the woman of many nuances. The curatorial dualism is methodically transferred here into the picture, thus culminating in synthesis. ROSA is equally coherent and graceful, both present and absent. Far from being naïve and insipid, ROSA is well calculated and sensitively thought out.
ROSA is no prototype.
Not pink, but a transformative figure who can be many individuals in one person.

1 Ingeborg Bachmann, *Malina*, translated by Philip Boehm, New York, 1990.
2 Caroline Kaufmann, *Zur Semantik der Farbadjektive rosa, pink und rot*, Munich, 2006, p. 35.
3 Ibid. p. 74.
4 Ibid. p. 67.

„ … WO WIR SIE ERWARTEN.“

Malerei und Teamwork

Doris Krystof

Der große Theoretiker der Malerei der Postmoderne, der französisch-algerische Kunsthistoriker Yve-Alain Bois, beschließt seinen Aufsatz *Malerei als Trauerarbeit* (1990) mit einem Hinweis auf Robert Musil, der in den 1940er Jahren konstatierte, dass „(…) die Malerei, die Maler, wenn es sie denn noch geben wird, nicht von dorther kommen werden, wo wir sie erwarten“[1].

Das hört sich nach melancholisch-weiser Voraussicht an, gleichzeitig belegt Musils Überlegung die enorme kulturphilosophische Aufladung des Mediums Malerei, das in der Geschichte vielfach als Gradmesser für zivilisatorische Zustände und den gesellschaftlichen Fortschritt herhalten musste. Dass man zu Musils Zeit – die, wie Bois ausführlich beschreibt, auch Piet Mondrians Zeit und damit die der abstrakten Malerei ist – die Existenz von Malerinnen unterschlägt, lässt schon ahnen, aus welcher Richtung, mehr oder weniger unerwartet, für den Fortbestand der Malerei gesorgt werden könnte. Heute ist die ehemals männliche Dominanz in der nach wie vor höchst vitalen und beliebten Gattung Malerei zwar nicht abgeschafft, aber doch stark gemindert. Das belegt der Erfolg von Künstlerinnen wie Tomma Abts, Monika Baer, Vija Celmins, Marlene Dumas oder Nicole Eisenman, um nur einige wenige Beispiele aus einer wachsenden Reihe zu nennen, zu der auch junge Positionen wie Rosilene Luduvico und Sabrina Fritsch beitragen.

Die Malerei ist nicht nur die am häufigsten totgesagte und sich immer wieder neu erfindende Gattung in der bildenden Kunst, sondern die Malerei hält auch, prägnant und zäh zugleich, am Bestehen individueller Autorschaft fest. Zwar ist es im Zuge der Kritik an dem genialischen Konzept aus der Zeit der Romantik sowie durch die Kraft kollaborativer Praktiken in der Kunst seit den 1980er Jahren auch im Bereich der Malerei vereinzelt und bisweilen durchaus strategisch zu Teamwork gekommen (man denke etwa an Martin Kippenberger und Albert Oehlen). Beispiele kooperierender Malerinnen hingegen lassen sich kaum finden, sieht man von der berühmten Ausnahme von der Regel ab, die in den unter dem Label *Free Time* zusammen malenden New Yorker Künstlerinnen Jutta Koether, Rita Ackerman und Kim Gordon besteht.[2] Überhaupt scheint die künstlerische Zusammenarbeit eher in der Konstellation von zwei Männern oder eines weiblich/männlichen Paares zu funktionieren. Angefangen bei Bernd und Hilla Becher bis zu Elmgreen und Dragset sind in der Kunstgeschichte der letzten vier Jahrzehnte zahlreiche künstlerische Zweierbeziehungen zu fassen, während als dauerhaft zusammenarbeitende weibliche Teams allenfalls Schwestern kooperieren. Das belegen Beispiele wie Irene und Christine Hohenbüchler, Jane und Louise Wilson oder Claudia und Julia Müller, die alle möglichen künstlerischen Praktiken verfolgen, aber nicht die Malerei.

Häufiger kommt es hingegen vor, dass zwei Künstlerinnen gemeinsam ausstellen. Entweder steht dabei eine kuratorische Idee dahinter, die darauf abzielt, eine inhaltliche oder formale Verbindung der beiden Positionen zu verdeutlichen und aus dem Kontrast womöglich neue Einsichten zu generieren. Oder aber die Doppelausstellung geht von den Künstlerinnen selbst aus, um das Eigene durch das Andere im Sinne von Synergie oder Synthese zu erforschen und etwa zur gemeinsamen Durchsetzung einer neuen künstlerischen Haltung zu verstärken. Was die bislang einmalige Kooperation von Rosilene Luduvico und Sabrina Fritsch in der Ausstellung bei Philara Ende des Jahres 2015 betrifft, ging die gegenseitige Annäherung noch einen Schritt weiter, denn mit einigen Details im Umfeld der Ausstellung wurde angedeutet, es könnte sich bei den ausgestellten Arbeiten um die künstlerische Produktion *einer* Person handeln. Das legte zumindest die Einladungskarte nahe, die das Gesicht einer Frau zeigte, während der Pressetext unter Verwendung eines Zitats aus Ingeborg Bachmanns Roman *Malina* verkündete: „In ROSA, der letzten Ausstellung der Sammlung Philara in den Ausstellungsräumen in Reisholz, laden die Künstlerinnen Sabrina Fritsch und Rosilene Luduvico ein zur Erkundung ‚der Legende einer Frau, die es nie gegeben hat‘“.[3]

Mit der österreichischen Schriftstellerin Ingeborg Bachmann wurde ausgerechnet eine Künstlerin aufgerufen, die wie kaum jemand sonst in der Moderne für eine solipsistische, das heißt rein auf sich selbst bezogene Kunst steht. Für eine Kunst, die aus sich selbst schöpft und sich vollständig unfähig (und unwillig) zu jeglicher Kooperation erweist, wie man aus Bachmanns hartnäckiger Weigerung weiß, für den Komponisten Hans Werner Henze trotz dessen Flehen ein Libretto zu schreiben. Ganz anders die Malerinnen Sabrina Fritsch und Rosilene Luduvico, die zumindest für die Dauer einer Ausstellung probeweise ihre Stimmen zum Duett erhoben, um in zwei unterschiedlichen, aber nicht ganz und gar differenten Tonlagen ein Konzert zur Aufführung zu bringen. Gemeinsam ist den beiden Absolventinnen der Düsseldorfer Kunstakademie nämlich, tief in das historische Repertoire der Malerei der Moderne zu greifen und damit einer der ältesten der Künste neues Leben einzuhauchen. Wobei Rosilene Luduvico mit zehn Jahren Vorsprung ihre zarte informell-gestische Malerei und Zeichnung bereits mehrfach in einer durch Teamwork erprobten künstlerischen Praxis weiter entwickelt hat, während Sabrina Fritsch mit ihren nachdrücklichen Paraphrasen auf die geometrische Abstraktion in der von ihr angeregten Doppelausstellung den Weg einer autonom betriebenen Malerei zum ersten Mal verlassen hat.

Die Kooperation der Malerinnen bei Philara bestand zunächst aus Auswahl und Arrangement von elf im Raum verteilten Zusammenstellungen von zwei (einmal drei) Arbeiten, wobei jeweils die eine von Rosilene Luduvico und die andere von Sabrina Fritsch stammte. Die Zusammenarbeit gipfelte in der gemeinsam vor Ort gefertigten und der Ausstellung den Titel gebenden Wandarbeit *ROSA*. Das Akronym, das sich unschwer als aus den ersten Silben der Vornamen der beiden Künstlerinnen zusammengesetzt zu erkennen gibt, folgt dem kombinierenden Prinzip des surrealistischen Cadavre Exquis. Mit seiner willkürlich künstlerischen Kombinatorik verweist es nicht nur auf das von Rosilene Luduvico und Sabrina Fritsch erprobte Verfahren der Zusammenstellung ihrer Gemälde, sondern kam auch bei der Gestaltung des Motivs für die Einladungskarte mit der frontalen Aufnahme eines weiblichen Gesichts zur Anwendung. Denn bei dem Foto handelte es sich um eine Montage aus den beiden Gesichtshälften der Künstlerinnen, wobei die horizontale Schnittstelle wie bei den berühmten surrealistischen Gruppenzeichnungen nicht überarbeitet oder kaschiert war. Vielmehr wurde die Trennlinie zwischen oberer (Sabrinas) und unterer (Rosilenes) Gesichtshälfte durch den Falz der Klappkarte so stark betont, dass „die Legende einer Frau, die es nie gegeben hat“ schnell zu durchschauen war. Tatsächlich ging es bei dem Kooperationsprojekt ROSA weniger um ein Verwirrspiel der Identitäten als um die Erkundung einer zuvor nicht erkannten Verwandtschaft zwischen zwei künstlerischen Positionen und womöglich um ein den Surrealisten abgeschautes, den künstlerischen Prozess produktiv steuerndes Spiel mit dem Zufall.

Durch die betont dichte Hängung der Bilderpaare wurden stichprobenhaft und spielerisch unterschiedlich ausdeutbare Bezugnahmen vorgeführt; es war, als würden sich zwei malerische Subjekte versuchsweise einmal zusammenlegen, um exemplarisch die gegenseitige Wirkung ihrer Bilder aufeinander zu testen und womöglich daraus ganz im Sinne surrealistischer Kombinatorik Funken zu schlagen. Trotz aller Verschiedenheit traten Ähnlichkeiten zutage. Am deutlichsten zeigte das die Kombination, bei der mit Sabrina Fritschs *alop (FP)* und Rosilene Luduvicos *Eira* zwei nahezu gleich große Gemälde gegenübergestellt wurden. Jedes der beiden 2013 entstandenen Bilder charakterisiert ein kleinteiliges Allover auf hellem Grund; *alop (FP)* ist mit dem Konstrukt einer an Agnes Martins frühe Kompositionen erinnernden, zarten Rasterstruktur besetzt, während bei *Eira* ein dynamischer Strudel aus kurzen pastellfarbenen Pinselstrichen über die Leinwand zieht. In einer weiteren Kombination herrschte größte Differenz und erzeugte eine ganz andere, nahezu narrative Lesart der Bilder: Luduvicos kleinformatiges Gemälde eines wie zum Ruhen zur Seite geneigten Frauenkopfes, *Tico-tico* (24 x 31 cm), das entfernt an Alex Katz denken lässt, hing neben Sabrina Fritschs aus mehreren Spalten horizontaler Linien aufgebautem Großformat *Stst (acea)* (220 x 165 cm). Das Nebeneinander der Bilder bewirkte einen räumlichen Bezug und stellte im Auge des Betrachtenden eine Erzählung her. Erinnerte das horizontale Lineament doch an eine das Sonnenlicht abschirmende Jalousie, was zusammen mit der ruhenden Frau die Stimmung eines trägen Sommernachmittags evoziert, an dem ein vornehm blasses Gesicht Schutz vor der Hitze draußen sucht …

Mit dem Changieren zwischen Abstraktion und Figuration zielte die Doppelausstellung ROSA auf grundsätzliche Fragen der Lesbarkeit von Bildern ab. Dennoch gründete ROSA nicht auf einem in eingespielter Partnerschaft entwickelten theoretischen Konzept. Die projektbezogene Kooperation der beiden Malerinnen erprobte vielmehr eine neue Sicht auf die Malerei, bei der Kontext, Umgebung und Nachbarschaft des Gemäldes ebenso viel zählen wie Individualität, Autonomie und womöglich Aura. Indem Rosilene Luduvico und Sabrina Fritsch ihre Arbeiten selbst kuratierten und damit in einen Zusammenhang stellten, sorgten sie für eine Anschlussfähigkeit ihrer Bilder an das Œuvre der jeweils anderen. Rosilene Luduvico hatte diese Art von Anschlussfähigkeit durch Teamwork bereits mit anderen Künstlern wie den Japanern Hiroshi Sugito und Takeshi Makishima mehrfach erprobt. Sie hat dabei als Malerin immer wieder andere Vorgehensweisen getestet und damit die eigene Position einer dezenten poetischen Malerei gestärkt. Bei einer Performance mit dem Musiker Hauschka im Kunstverein Schwerte (2011) konzentrierte sich ihr Beitrag als Malerin auf einen Wimpernschlag, in dem ihr berückendes Augenmakeup in funkelndem Smaragdgrün für einen kurzen Moment zum Vorschein kam, um dann wieder der Musik den Vortritt zu lassen.

Dass Teamwork aus dem Rhythmus von Geben, Nehmen, Zurückgeben und Zurücknehmen besteht, kam schließlich in der gemeinsamen Wandmalerei *ROSA* zum Ausdruck. Auf der Stirnseite eines abgetrennten kleineren Raums in der Ausstellung entstand ein leicht Sabrina Fritsch zuzuordnendes rechteckiges Feld, das aus acht Reihen von alternierend schwarzen und weißen kleineren rechteckigen Formen zusammengesetzt war. Die Setzung einer plakativen Rasterformation in den Nichtfarben Schwarz und Weiß, die mit einigen Unregelmäßigkeiten selbst schon eine Aufgabe der reinen Lehre der geometrischen Abstraktion betrieb, wurde von Rosilene Luduvico insofern vollends konterkariert, als sie die grafische Struktur mit wie beiläufig aufgetragenen, weit über das Raster in den Raum ausgreifenden bunten Farbspritzern überzogen hat. In dieser Kombination offenbarte sich schließlich noch einmal das surreale Prinzip von ROSA als ein Zusammentreffen von zwei jeweils eigenständig an der Moderne geschulten, die Moderne beschwörenden und gleichermaßen torpedierenden, freigeistigen Künstlerinnen, die aus dem Abstand zwischen ihnen einen produktiven Bereich des Dazwischen entwickelten.

1 Yve-Alain Bois, "Malerei als Trauerarbeit", in ders., *Painting as Model* (1990), hier zitiert nach: *The Happy Fainting of Painting. Ein Reader zur zeitgenössischen Malerei*, hg. von Hans-Jürgen Hafner und Gunter Reski, Köln 2014, S. 46.
2 Zur Konjunktur kooperativer Praktiken in der Gegenwartskunst am Ende des 20. Jahrbhunderts vgl. *Get Together. Kunst als Teamwork*. Ausst.-Kat. Kunsthalle Wien 1999.
3 Der Pressetext der Ausstellung weist das Zitat nach als: Ingeborg Bachmann, *Malina*, Frankfurt/Main 1980.

"… WHERE WE EXPECT THEM"
Painting and Teamwork

Doris Krystof

The French-Algerian art historian Yve-Alain Bois, a great theoretician of painting in the postmodern era, concludes his essay *Painting: The Task of Mourning* (1990) with a reference to Robert Musil who in the 1940s had asserted that "(…) if some painting is still to come, if painters are still to come, they will not come from where we expect them to."[1]

That sounds like a wise, melancholy forecast, yet Musil's observation simultaneously underlines the highly charged cultural-philosophical medium of painting that, time and again throughout history, served as a barometer for civilised conditions and social progression. When Musil was alive, as Bois describes in detail, it was also the era of Piet Mondrian and abstract painting; however, given the suppression of female painters at that time it is not difficult to guess from which direction, as it were virtually unawares, the next generation could emerge to assure the future of painting. Today, the earlier dominance of male artists in the ever vibrant and popular genre of painting may not have been entirely lifted, yet it has substantially diminished. This is evidenced by the success of female artists like Tomma Abts, Monika Baer, Vija Celmins, Marlene Dumas or Nicole Eisenman to name just a few artists among a growing number that also includes recent contributions from young artists like Rosilene Luduvico and Sabrina Fritsch.

In the visual arts, painting is not only the most frequently written off and most repeatedly reinvented genre but it also retains, distinctively and tenaciously, the persistence of individual authorship. In the wake of the Romantic period and its critique of the concept of artistic genius as well as through the power of collaborative practices in art since the 1980s, it is true that sporadic examples have come to the fore in painting and occasional cases of highly strategic teamwork (one thinks of Martin Kippenberger and Albert Oehlen). On the other hand, hardly any models of collaborative projects emerge with female artists, if one overlooks the famous exception to the rule in New York, known as *Free Time* with artists painting together, like Jutta Koether, Rita Ackerman and Kim Gordon.[2] In general, the constellation of two men or the artist duo of one woman/one man seems to be the functional basis for collaborations. Beginning with Bernd and Hilla Becher to Elmgreen and Dragset, the last four decades of art history incorporate numerous artistic double acts, while women artist teams at best collaborate in the long run as sisters. Think of artist duos like Irene and Christine Hohenbüchler, Jane and Louise Wilson or Claudia and Julia Müller who pursue all kinds of artistic techniques, but not painting.

By contrast, two female artists more usually exhibit their work in tandem. The motivation for this is either a curatorial idea aimed at highlighting an association based on the content or formal aspects of both positions, and possibly to generate new insights from the juxtaposition. Alternatively, the artists initiate the joint exhibition to explore their personal work through the other in the sense of synergy or synthesis and, for instance, to accentuate and jointly assert a new artistic approach. Regarding the previously one-off collaborative project by Rosilene Luduvico and Sabrina Fritsch in the exhibition at the Philara Collection at the end of 2015, the mutual rapprochement advanced a step further. Indeed, some accompanying details for the exhibition suggested that the works on display might offer the artistic production *of a single* person. At least, this was implied by the invitation card depicting a woman's face, while the press release borrowed a quotation from Ingeborg Bachmann's novel *Malina*, as follows: "In ROSA, the last Philara Collection exhibition in the rooms at Reisholz, the artists Sabrina Fritsch and Rosilene Luduvico invite you to explore 'the legend of a woman who never existed.'"[3]

The quotation from the Austrian writer Ingeborg Bachmann defers to an artist who was unrivalled in the modernist age for representing solipsistic, that is, purely self-referential art. In other words, art with its internal creative source and wholly incapable (and unwilling) of engaging in any cooperation. This is well known from Bachmann's stubborn refusal, despite the entreaties, to write a libretto for composer Hans Werner Henze. The situation is totally different for the painters Sabrina Fritsch and Rosilene Luduvico who at least for the run of an exhibition gave a concert performance of an experimental duet raising their voices in two contrasted, yet not entirely different tonalities. The common element for both graduates of the Düsseldorf Art Academy is to delve deep into the historical repertoire of modernist painting, and so to breathe new life into one of the oldest arts. Thanks to her lead of ten years' experience, Rosilene Luduvico had already refined her gentle, informal and gestural painting and drawing through several trial runs of artistic teamwork. On the other hand, with her emphatic paraphrases on geometric abstraction, in Sabrina Fritsch's self-initiated joint exhibition she first strayed from the path of autonomous painting.

The artists' collaborative work at Philara initially involved a selection and arrangement placed in the room of eleven compositions in two (and a unique set of three) works that originated respectively from Rosilene Luduvico, while the other was created by Sabrina Fritsch. The jointly created wall mural and the exhibition's namesake – *ROSA* – was the culmination of the collaborative project. The acronym, which is clearly derived from the initial syllables of the artists' first names, follows the combining principle of surrealist *cadavre exquis* drawing. Its bizarre style of artistic assemblage not only implies the tried and tested technique adopted by Rosilene Luduvico and Sabrina Fritsch of combining their paintings, but was also the basis of the motif design for the invitation card with the front view of a female face. The photo materialised as a montage of both halves of the artists' faces with the horizontal interface not being reworked or concealed, as in the famous surrealist group drawings. Rather, the demarcation line between the top (Sabrina's) and bottom (Rosilene's) half of the face was so heavily accentuated due to the fold in the card that one could quickly see through "the legend of a woman who never existed". The collaborative project ROSA was less about a deliberate confusion of identities than about exploring a hitherto non-identified relationship between two artistic positions, and perhaps about emanating the surrealists' play with the accidental that productively steers the artistic process.

The obviously concentrated display of picture pairs in a random and playful way helped to demonstrate a variety of explanatory references. It was as though two painterly subjects would tentatively join forces for a one-off and exemplary test of the mutual effect of their paintings, and possibly to throw off sparks entirely in keeping with surrealist combinations. Despite all the differences, similarities came to light. The clearest example here was the version in which two almost identically sized paintings were combined: Sabrina Fritsch's *alop (FP)* and Rosilene Luduvico's *Eira*. Each of the works (dating from 2013) is characterised by a fragmented all-over painting on a light background; *alop (FP)* is filled with the construct of a delicate grid structure evoking Agnes Martin's early compositions, while *Eira* is composed of a dynamic maelstrom of short pastel-coloured brushstrokes across the canvas. Another combination was governed by the greatest difference and produced an entirely contrastive, almost narrative interpretation of the pictures: Luduvico's small-format portrait of a woman's head inclined to one side as though resting, *Tico-tico* (24 x 31 cm), which is vaguely reminiscent of Alex Katz, was displayed alongside Sabrina Fritsch's large format *Stst (acea)* (220 x 165 cm) and composed of several columns of horizontal lines. The pictures' coexistence produced a spatial relationship and represented a narrative from the viewer's perspective. Indeed, the horizontal linear character was reminiscent of shade-giving sun blinds, and together with the resting woman conjured up the atmosphere of a lethargic summer afternoon when a fine-featured, pale face seeks protection from the heat outside…

With the alternation from abstraction to figuration the joint exhibition ROSA addressed fundamental questions of the readability of paintings. Nevertheless, ROSA was not founded on a theoretical concept developed through the practice of partnership. Rather, both artists' project-focused collaboration tested a novel perception of painting where the context, environment and neighbourhood of a painting counts just as much as individuality, autonomy and perhaps also aura. By curating their own artworks, and thus placing them in a specific context, Rosilene Luduvico und Sabrina Fritsch ensured their paintings gained connectivity with the respective other artist's œuvre. On several previous occasions, Rosilene Luduvico had tried this form of connectivity through teamwork with other artists like the Japanese artists Hiroshi Sugito and Takeshi Makishima. As a painter, she repeatedly experimented with other approaches, thereby strengthening her own position of discreetly poetic painting style. In a performance with the musician Hauschka at the Kunstverein Schwerte (2011), her contribution as a painter was focused on a blink of an eye when her captivating, glittering emerald green eye make-up momentarily came to the fore and then allowed the music to take centre stage again.

Ultimately, the collaborative wall mural ROSA expressed how teamwork can consist of the rhythm of giving, taking, giving back and taking back. On the facing side of a smaller, partitioned room at the exhibition an upright rectangular field was created – easily attributable to Sabrina Fritsch – comprising eight rows of alternating black and white smaller, upright rectangular forms. The placing of a striking grid formation in the non-colours black and white – with several irregularities, it already posed a problem in pure geometric abstraction theory – was fully counteracted by Rosilene Luduvico to the extent that she overdrew the graphic structure with seemingly arbitrarily applied bright colour splashes reaching far beyond the grid and into the room. Ultimately, the surreal principle of ROSA was again exposed in this combination as an encounter between two artists. Each artist had trained independently in modernist painting and each acclaimed modernism while torpedoing it. At the same time they had turned the distance between them into a productive area of the *in-between*.

1 Yve-Alain Bois, "Painting: The Task of Mourning", in idem, *Painting as Model* (Cambridge, Massachusetts, 1993), p. 244.
2 On the buoyant activity of collaborative practices in late 20th century contemporary art, see *Get Together. Kunst als Teamwork.* Exhibition Catalogue (Kunsthalle Vienna, 1999).
3 The press release for the exhibition cites the quotation from Ingeborg Bachmann's *Malina* (English transl. by Philip Boehm, New York, 1990).

Rosilene Luduvico

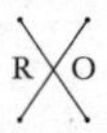

cat. 2
Inclinado 2009
Öl auf Kreide auf Leinen /
Oil on chalk on linen
94 x 69 cm
Courtesy Rosilene Luduvico und Galerie Zink, Waldkirchen in der Oberpfalz

cat. 3
Tico-tico 2009
Öl auf Kreide auf Leinen /
Oil on chalk on linen
24 x 31 cm
Courtesy Rosilene Luduvico und Galerie Zink, Waldkirchen in der Oberpfalz

cat. 6
Silenzio 2010
Öl auf Kreide auf Nessel /
Oil on chalk on cotton
30,5 x 23 cm
Sammlung / Collection Rainer Haarmann, Berlin

cat. 8
For you and for me 2014
Öl auf Kreide auf Leinen /
Oil on chalk on linen
32 x 25 cm
Sammlung / Collection Rainer Haarmann, Berlin

cat. 9
For Macunaíma 2011
Öl auf Kreide auf Leinen /
Oil on chalk on linen
112 x 145 cm
Courtesy Rosilene Luduvico und Galerie Zink, Waldkirchen in der Oberpfalz

cat. 11
Esther 2016
Öl auf Kreide auf Leinen /
Oil on chalk on linen
40 x 30 cm
Privatsammlung / Private collection Berlin

cat. 13
Seine erste Reise 2014
Öl auf Kreide auf Leinen /
Oil on chalk on linen
33 x 24 cm
Privatsammlung / Private collection Parsberg

cat. 15
Touch 2016
Öl auf Kreide auf Leinen /
Oil on chalk on linen
35 x 30 cm
Sammlung Philara, Düsseldorf

cat. 17
Das letzte Gespräch 2010
Öl auf Kreide auf Leinen /
Oil on chalk on linen
30,5 x 23 cm
Courtesy Rosilene Luduvico und Galerie Zink, Waldkirchen in der Oberpfalz

cat. 20
Eira 2013
Öl auf Kreide auf Leinen /
Oil on chalk on linen
33 x 26 cm
Courtesy Rosilene Luduvico und Galerie Zink, Waldkirchen in der Oberpfalz

cat. 21
Credi 2013
Öl auf Kreide auf Leinen /
Oil on chalk on linen
27 x 22 cm
Privatsammlung / Private collection São Paulo

cat. 23
Zeitkapsel 2010
Öl auf Leinwand /
Oil on canvas
18 x 24 cm
Sammlung / Collection Reydan Weiss

cat. 26
Chichia 2015
Öl auf Kreide auf Leinen /
Oil on chalk on linen
190 x 170 cm
Courtesy Rosilene Luduvico und Galerie Zink, Waldkirchen in der Oberpfalz

Sabrina Fritsch

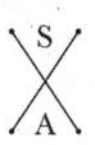

cat. 1
zange 2012
Öl, Tusche auf Acryl auf Baumwolle /
Oil, Indian ink on acrylic on cotton
52 x 41 cm
Privatsammlung / Private collection

cat. 4
Stst (acea) 2013
Öl, Acryl auf Rupfen auf Leinwand /
Oil, acrylic on hessian on canvas
220 x 165 cm
Courtesy Sabrina Fritsch und VAN HORN,
Düsseldorf

cat. 5
ior 2012
Öl, Acryl auf Rupfen auf Baumwolle /
Oil, acrylic on hessian on cotton
60 x 47 cm
Alpine Collection

cat. 7
acco 2015
Öl, Acryl, Bleistift auf Jute /
Oil, acrylic, pencil on burlap
200 x 160 cm
Museum Kunstpalast, Düsseldorf

cat. 10
mounZ 2016
Öl, Acryl auf Rupfen auf Baumwolle auf Holz /
Oil, acrylic on hessian on canvas on wood
30 x 25 cm
Courtesy Sabrina Fritsch und VAN HORN,
Düsseldorf

cat. 12
lioht 2016
Öl, Acryl, Tusche auf Baumwolle /
Oil, acrylic, Indian ink on cotton
250 x 180 cm
FPM Collection, Viersen

cat. 14
acea 2015
Öl, Acryl auf Rupfen auf Leinwand /
Oil, acrylic on hessian on canvas
80 x 56 cm
Courtesy Sabrina Fritsch und VAN HORN,
Düsseldorf

cat. 16
Zoa 2016
Öl, Acryl auf Jute /
Oil, acrylic on burlap
280 x 200 cm
Sammlung Philara, Düsseldorf

cat. 18
enwu 2012
Öl auf Baumwolle /
Oil on cotton
60 x 47 cm
Sammlung Philara, Düsseldorf

cat. 19
alop (FP) 2013
Öl, Acryl auf Rupfen auf Leinwand /
Oil, acrylic on hessian on canvas
35 x 28 cm
Sammlung / Collection Helga Meister

cat. 22
Cafor 2015
Acryl auf Rupfen auf Leinwand /
Acrylic on hessian on canvas
200 x 160 cm
Courtesy Sabrina Fritsch und VAN HORN,
Düsseldorf

cat. 24
lauor 2013
Öl auf Baumwolle /
Oil on cotton
60 x 47 cm
Courtesy Sabrina Fritsch und VAN HORN,
Düsseldorf

cat. 25
mons 2011
Öl auf Baumwolle /
Oil on cotton
52 x 41 cm
Sammlung Philara, Düsseldorf

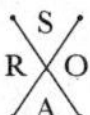

cat. 27
ROSA 2015
Aquarell und Acryl auf Wand /
Watercolour and acrylic mural
338 x 288 cm
Gemeinschaftsarbeit / Collective work
Sammlung Philara, Düsseldorf

Herausgeber & Konzept / Editors & Concept:
Sabrina Fritsch, Rosilene Luduvico
Texte / Texts: Katharina Klang, Dr. Doris Krystof
Übersetzung / Translation: Dr. Suzanne Kirkbright
Lektorat / Copy Editing: Doris Lösch

Fotografie / Photography:
Achim Kukulies, Düsseldorf
außer / except cat. 10 : Tamara Lorenz, Köln
Gestaltung / Design: Adeline Morlon
Bildbearbeitung / Image Editing: Henning Krause

Gesamtherstellung / Production:
DZA Druckerei zu Altenburg GmbH

Veröffentlicht in einer limitierten Auflage von /
Published in a limited edition of 500

Vertrieb / Distribution: Gestalten, Berlin,
www.gestalten.com, sales@gestalten.com

ISBN 978-3-95476-191-3

Printed in Germany

Erschienen im / Published by
DISTANZ Verlag, www.distanz.de

Gefördert durch die / Funded by

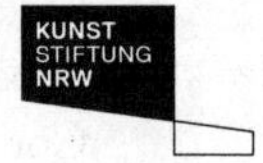

Mit freundlicher Unterstützung der /
With kind support of

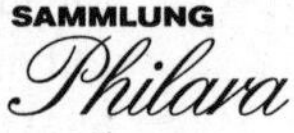

Galerie Zink, Waldkirchen in der Oberpfalz
und / and VAN HORN, Düsseldorf

Besonderer Dank / Special Thanks:
Gil Bronner, Katharina Klang, Henning Krause, Doris Krystof,
Achim Kukulies, Doris Lösch, Adeline Morlon, Cynthia Pauls,
Daniela Steinfeld, Michael Zink,
allen Sammlern / all collectors und unseren Helden / and our heroes

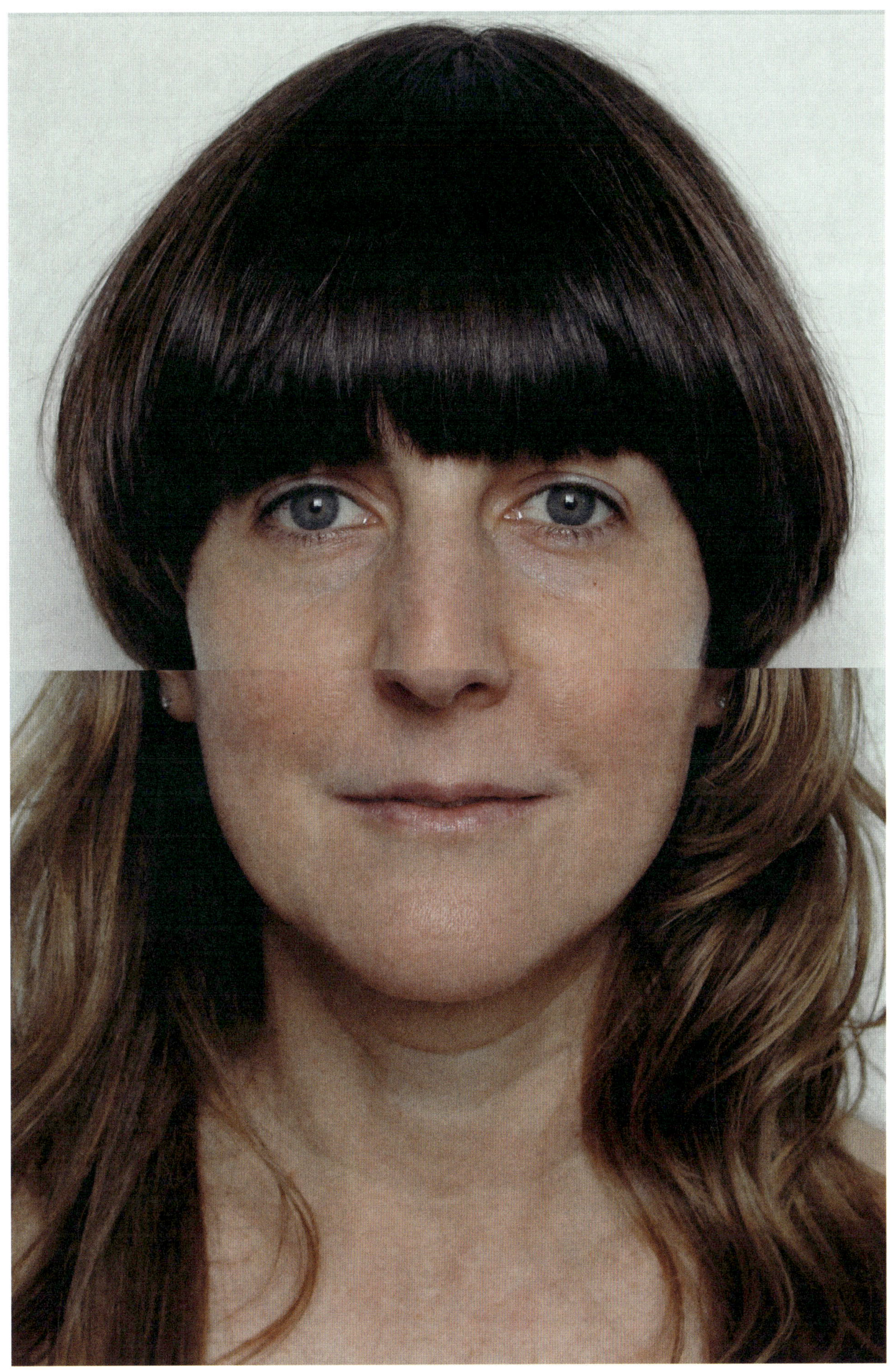

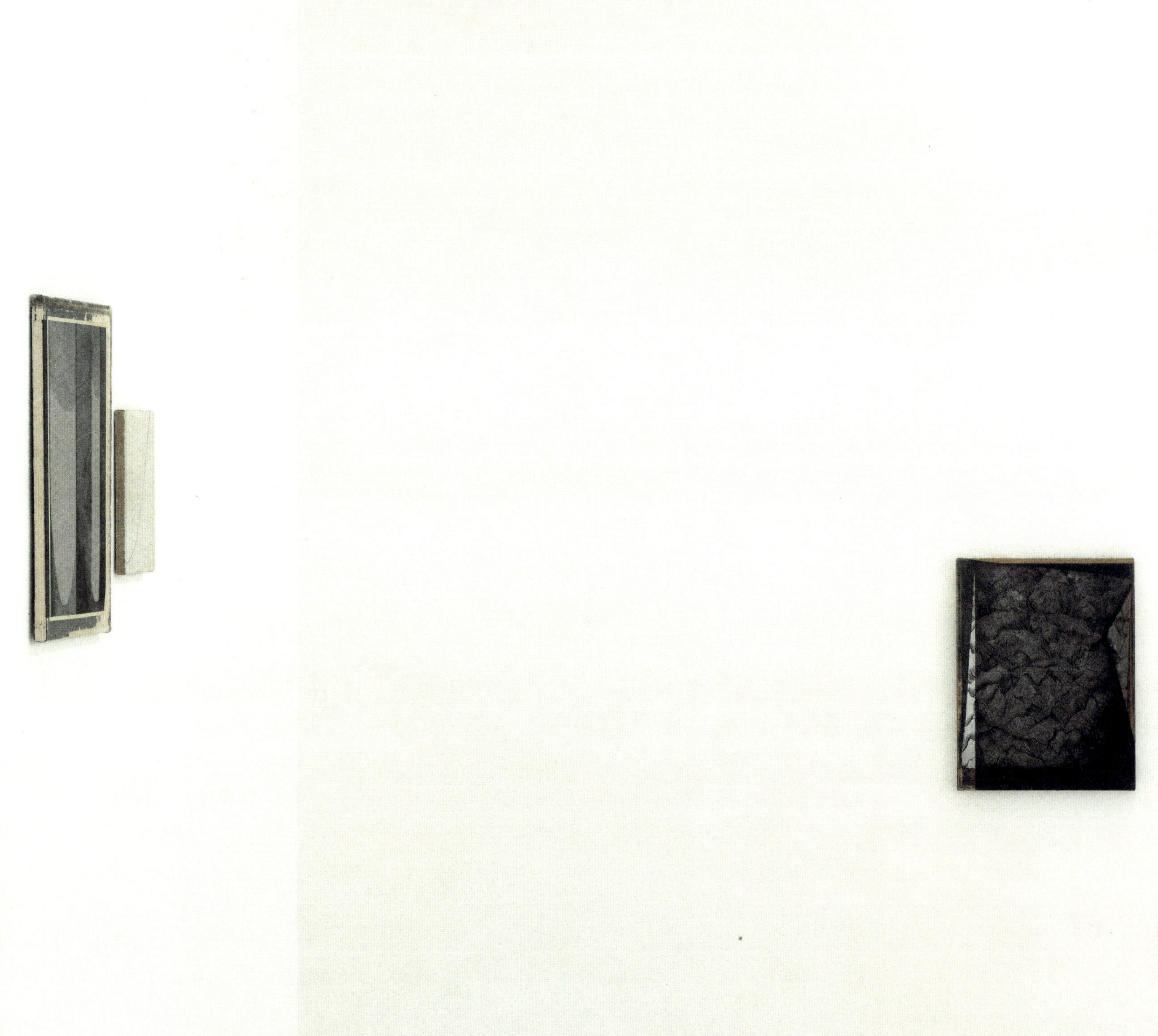